THE SELFISH CAREER

How to Bend the Rules in Your Favor, Make Extra Money, and Get More from Your Company Than They Get from You

BY MATTHEW D TUCKER

Copyright © 2019 by Matthew David Tucker and
Breakthrough Holdings, LLC

All rights reserved. This book may not be reproduced in whole or in part without written permission from the publisher, except by a reviewer who may quote brief passages in a review; nor may any part of this book be reproduced, stored in a retrieval system, or transmitted in any form or by any means, electronic, mechanical, photocopying, recording, or other, without written permission from the copyright holder.

Ebook ASIN: B07V9LB3MQ
Paperback ASIN: 1080859438
Paperback ISBN: 9781080859436

ACKNOWLEDGMENTS

To Amy, who always supports my crazy and nutty ideas and has never asked me to be like everyone else. In fact, you have loved me because I don't do those things. I'm lucky I'm in love with my best friend.

To Jackson, at 14, you're very patient at listening to my thoughts and advice. Way more than I was at your age. That's a good thing. I wish I'd listened to Papa more often. If you will, I'm sure you won't have as rough a road as I have. I love you more than you know.

And for my grandmother, who always told me I could do anything I set my mind to.

CREDITS

A huge thanks goes to Shannon Constantine Logan (shannon.constantine@gmail.com) for partnering with me to finish this book. You took it from an 8 to an 11!

TABLE OF CONTENTS

Introduction

Chapter I: Don't Be a Good Corporate Citizen

Chapter II: Don't be a Corporate Drone, Your Career is a Complex Game You Have to Play

Chapter III: Don't Get Distracted by Promotions, Build Skills Instead

Chapter IV: Never Share Your True Feelings or Ultimate Agenda

Chapter V: Don't Invest in "Low ROI" Internal Relationships, Focus on High Return External Ones

Chapter VI: Never Bring Someone else's Idea to Reality

Chapter VII: Don't Get Caught Without a Long Term Plan

Chapter VIII: When in Doubt, Tell People What to Do

Chapter IX: Abandon Ship when the Company is Sinking

Chapter X: You Can't Fix a Bad Boss...So Don't Bother

Chapter XI: Your Brand is More Important than Your Company's

Chapter XII: Final Words of Advice...

INTRODUCTION

No one has ever accused me of being average, but I'm not a multi-millionaire CEO that runs some massive business or invented the latest exciting new tech. I'm not an executive at Google writing a book because I'm going to tell you something "inspired" that I never did myself.

I've had some big wins. But I've also made some seriously stupid mistakes in my career.

I had a slow start to my career. Going to college was expected of me, and while I've always wanted to learn, none of the majors inspired me. After bombing out of pharmacy school, switching majors, and working (briefly) as a chemist, I found myself in a dead-end IT job, wasting years playing more golf than I actually spent time working. One day I woke up and started having panic attacks and realized how dissatisfied I was with my life and career. I call this my "quarter-life crisis." I was 26 years old.

So, I went back to get my MBA and picked the tough route: night classes from the ground up with all the prerequisites. This time I wanted to learn.

My focus was in global finance, and I loved it. But when I graduated, I realized in order to work in finance, I would have to move to New York to get a job at any of the investment banks. Moving wasn't an option, so I went with something familiar and closer to home...I took a job in sales at a big multi-national medical device company. It was the first time I was proud of my job, but by the time I had a career that made me feel like I was successful, I was 29. I'd wasted 8 years and felt far behind everyone else.

After a couple years in sales, I was able to transfer to our corporate office in Chicago into a product strategy and marketing role. I was on a mission to make up for the lost time. Out of the seven years I was there, I was promoted six times. I just kept moving up the food chain. But the business started missing its financial goals, and suddenly what had been my ideal dream job turned into a nightmare.

The thing about when a company must do a turnaround is that you can survive them, but the journey is so miserable that it isn't worth getting to the destination. I'd never been through anything like this before, and I was fiercely loyal to my leadership, so I decided to stick it out. During this time, I was getting more opportunities and promotions. I thought only about the best-case scenario...that I'd keep moving up. At first, things looked optimistic, but it rapidly went south, and I learned that some decisions are even out of the leadership's hands.

The company was under a DOJ investigation in another business unit, but the scrutiny extended to our unrelated group. Sales and marketing team members were hauled into meetings with HR and legal multiple times a week. People started clawing and scratching at each other, trying to hang onto their jobs, and it got ugly. Executives would be flown into corporate and given their walking papers the same day for 'violations.' Nearly every week, I was being asked to 'give the background' on these situations, forced to put my job security in front of being a good person and supporting my colleagues. It was the most stressful situation you could imagine, and I lived with a lot of guilt. The lawyers were confrontational, and they assumed you did something wrong, so you were always on the defensive. They always said, 'We're just doing our job.'

Finally, one day, after five or six months of living in constant fear, they called me into the office in the middle of the day. The meeting started off just like the others, with a seemingly innocuous question. "What do you know about our policy on entertainment?"

Then the lawyer asked, "Can you explain why you spent $75 on a bottle of red wine?"

My neck got hot, I felt like I was back in second grade being scolded. "When?"

They pushed a piece of paper across the table at me, it was a printout of an old expense account. It was from four years ago. You see, there was a new policy that you couldn't spend more than $65 on a bottle of wine, and I had violated a policy *four years ago* – the policy hadn't even been created yet. This was the nuttiest accusation I'd ever heard of. It didn't make any sense. I looked at them and said, "Wait...you mean I was supposed to predict that you would create a policy four years in the future? That's fucked up." (In retrospect, I should have kept my mouth shut.)

Finally, it hit me. They were just looking for a reason, anything, so they could get rid of me. Not just me, but fire *anybody* who could be perceived as a problem. That way if the DOJ came in, they could say, "See! It was a rogue employee. We took immediate action." It was a shock they would accuse me of anything that wasn't above board. I used to partner with them in meetings to coach other team members on how to stay compliant and still grow the business.

I didn't handle the conversation well. I just couldn't understand; I'd been there so long. I touched nearly every piece of that business, and I'd led the massive growth of different brands. One of the first surgical products they gave me, I was able to double revenue in two years. I even won a cruise through the Mediterranean from the company for it. After that, they moved me to clean up another brand, I took over an acquisition the next year. I was tireless, I never stopped working. I loved the action.

In fact, I had put so much energy and time into my work, my marriage was circling the drain, and my job definitely wasn't making things better. I'd been spending half my time in the LA office—one week in Chicago, and one week in LA—for nearly two years. That didn't even include the other travel across the country I was doing, too.

The pressure didn't stop; it was six more months of these constant inquisitions. I started to nosedive. The lowest point was at our company annual meeting. I parked myself in front of the open bar that night and proceeded to get drunk and make an idiot out of myself in front of hundreds of my industry peers. Three months later, they wanted a "leadership change." I should have seen it coming. After all, a week earlier, they "Restructured" the department. My boss was laid off—and within days they got rid of my boss's replacement! These were good, dedicated people I respect to this day. That wasn't how they saw it, though. They were cleaning the house.

By 2013, I was wiped out financially after my layoff and divorce. Unfounded rumors circulated, and none of the recruiters would talk to me. It took two years to clear my name and set things right. I was living in a tiny one bedroom above a bar, starting from zero all over again. I kept wondering how I could work so hard and have nothing to show for it. I spent the next six years building myself back up to a place of abundance by helping big companies innovate and grow and by creating a successful consulting business that allowed me help others rapidly using all the things I've learned during my career. It wasn't easy.

But this was an important inflection point. I'd put so much into my job and held myself to such a high standard that they had to catch me in a minor slip up. It was the most ridiculous, humiliating, and infuriating moment of my career. Truly a "holy shit" moment. I came to the realization that these companies don't care. I learned an important lesson. Companies protect themselves at all costs.

I spent the next two years consulting independently with startups because I couldn't imagine working for a big company again. Although my business was successful, I got tired of the feast or famine lifestyle. When I got an offer from another multinational company, I told myself... *Ok, it's time to be selfish.*

This time I was much more calculating about how I approached the job. I developed skill sets I didn't have previously, and I did this at all costs, even if it meant I had to build the strategies into existing systems. For instance, I had no digital marketing experience, so I built "digital marketing strategy" into one of our brand plans so I could learn how to do it. I was also very vocal about pushing leadership to let me into the large enterprise strategy work groups so I could make better connections and show my skills of strategic thinking. I figured having a safety net of resources could be a benefit.

Also, another big one for me—I purposefully kept an inconsistent schedule. When you're consistent, everyone expects you to adhere to a standard 8-5, and they depend on you being there. They know that they can just walk down the hall and find you at every moment. But when nobody knows exactly when you're coming and going, you end up with more freedom and flexibility. I also traveled, but not as predictable as before. I tried new things and tested them, with an aim to get to a place where I could optimize my "selfish" career tactics and show others how to do it. Once I was confident the techniques worked, I started teaching my methods to others.

Having managed so many people over my career, I noticed common trends that hold individuals back from their full potential or their ability to make their jobs enjoyable and under their control. Most employees follow traditional career advice from books, blogs, or articles they've read on LinkedIn, and those strategies are locking them into a life where not only do they have limited options, but it also convinces them that there is safety where there is not, and loyalty where it doesn't exist.

The only way to break out of this cycle is to be what I call a "Rule Bender." Don't break the traditional rules—bend them in your favor. And if you don't, you accept becoming the corporate drones that companies love so much. The ones that tread water for years, and then get chewed up and spit out when times get rough or demoralized over time, so you accept any scraps others throw at you.

It's no secret that corporations show less and less loyalty to their employees year after year. We've all heard the stories from our parents or grandparents who started at a company when they were young and stayed there for decades. Maybe they worked for thirty years at a big company like Kraft, or PepsiCo, or on an assembly line at a car company. At worst they would make one or two moves to a different company within their career. It was expected that their companies would care for them and provide them with pensions, give them a true sense of security and stability, which allowed them to focus on their jobs and contribute to the bottom line.

It is a different world today. No longer are employees perceived as partners in your life. Companies manage to the bottom line and have to use any means at their disposal to protect their profitability and viability. Layoffs are common, reorganizations are routine, and working conditions are deteriorating. Healthcare benefits and retirement services continue to dwindle, costs are transferred to the employees, and pensions are nearly nonexistent. Cube farms and 'collaboration environments' pack employees into small spaces like sardines. Companies and managers brazenly tell employees they are "lucky to have a job," that "layoffs can happen anytime," or "you make too much money." In 2018, *the first comprehensive study* of the extreme pay gap between US executive suite and average workers was released and found, "[...] that the average CEO-to-worker pay ratio has now reached 339 to 1, with the highest pay gap approaching 5,000 to 1." That means it would take the average worker at the majority of these companies in the study 45 years to earn what their CEOs make in one year. (So, tell me again— who makes too much money?)

I don't blame them. I even admire the amazing focus that companies can drive from their employees, and the ability of very senior executives to dedicate their lives to a singular cause. But not everyone can do the same thing. If that sounds familiar, this book is for you.

Today, companies are using more resources than ever to paint a picture of an employee-centric and friendly working environment for recruitment and retention purposes. Simultaneously companies are less and less loyal, while they are increasing efforts to convince everyone they care. They actively manage the public's perception through social media, even going so far as to have employees speak on their behalf through social media. They organize and fund teams to campaign for awards in magazines about the best places to work. Despite these efforts, employees are posting candid reviews on Glassdoor to tell their cautionary tales and warn others. Most employees these days are resigned to job-hopping and simply 'Ghosting' jobs when they find a better one. According to 2012 US Department of Labor Statistics, 21% of average American workers now stay at their company less than twelve months, and the annual turnover rate is 19% (SHRM Human Capital Benchmarking Report). Company recruiters, for some reason, can't figure out why.

The above shows how companies act have Today and how often there is an infrastructure developed to limit opportunity, not cultivate it. This also conflicts with the nature of human relationships and causes a disconnect between perception and reality. There is an imbalance between the company loyalty, and the good loyalty people who work together need, and sometimes demand, from each other.

This creates an emotional tug-of-war between corporations and those in leadership positions. Leaders are responsible for productivity, retention, and staff development. Each employee's greatest source of feedback is from their manager, who has the responsibility to keep their role filled, stable, and productive. So, employees are often fooled into thinking their manager will take care of them and the company will listen to their manager's recommendations. Today, business leaders rarely teach the skills needed to navigate these difficult times simply because they aren't being incentivized to. In this situation, most employees find it very difficult to focus on doing what's right for themselves, their career, and their family.

My goal is to provide you with resources to cut through all the noise of "corporate propaganda" and determine what's real, so you know what is in your best interest. This book is to help you stay focused on what is best for you and provide tools you can use every day to maintain that focus. But it also gives you ways to be an asset to the organization.

What's inside this book will help you navigate career speed bumps and pitfalls to make sure you get the most out of your career and your company. Most important, it will allow each of your days at work to be driven by your choices. It will prevent your company from getting more from you than they give. As a result, you will be a greater asset to your company, but also a greater asset to *other* companies. As your overall value increases, this protects you against layoffs because if you do lose your job, you will be that much more confident about finding a new role quickly. Or you could even be inspired to build a side hustle or leave to create a business that could eventually free you from the shackles of corporate life forever.

I wrote this book to give people a pathway to making their career more about them and less about the needs of the companies they work for. But you have to do the work. Each chapter includes Take Home Summaries and an Action Item. These are to reinforce what you learned in each chapter, a task or two to engage you in a behavior or a mindset change to help you get out of your rut and commit to doing things differently than you are now.

Today, I am living proof of these strategies. I'm working at a job that I love that I've made about my goals, and not just what my company needs out of me. Everything is designed to help me more than it helps them even though I'm still providing them value and ideas few others can. This keeps my anxiety very low. I have control over my schedule (as I write this, I'm flying to Chicago for a board of directors meeting). I can simply say "I'm remote today" with no questions asked because of the problems I solve and growth I can deliver for the company. My wife and four kids have more than anyone could ever ask for; easily the top 0.5%. My life is filled with youth baseball and basketball games, gratifying work, friends, family vacations and time with my son, excursions to Europe or the Caribbean with my wife, and most importantly, <u>love</u>.

Will I ever be the CEO or president of a huge company someday? Nope. I'm sure of it....and I don't want to be. I'm a guy that enjoys working smarter, not harder. And that's what this book is all about: choices. Having more freedom of choices and building the experiences that let you live a life independent from corporations.

This book is for everyone who wakes up each morning wishing there was more. More from your company, more from your career, and more from your life. It's for everyone who wants to work hard, but is discouraged too often from doing so. It's for those that aren't good at the office politics and would rather succeed by succeeding so they don't end up faking their way into a job they aren't prepared to have.

I've tested and validated every step in this book, to help you navigate this new and challenging world, so you can create a life where you have options. I know this book will help you transform the approach to your career: but I hope most of all, it will transform your life.

CHAPTER I
DON'T BE A GOOD CORPORATE CITIZEN

Marie was one of the most dedicated salespeople I've ever seen, truly a force of nature. Mid-career, she jumped on a great opportunity to join a small company on the cusp of getting approval for a game-changing medical device. It was great timing, and she got in on the ground floor.

Marie's territory had almost no sales when she started, but in just a few years she had grown it to almost $8MM in revenue. Soon she was entrusted with training others in the field, and leading meetings within her region. She led the company's expansion into Canada, and her experience overcoming very different challenges in a new market made her even better at her job. Eventually, her success culminated in winning the President's Club and a trip to Italy as a reward.

Just a few months after her trip Marie was promoted to Regional Manager. But there was no time to rest on her laurels. At this same time, her company was being acquired by a much larger company who had their own way of doing things. Change management brought new expectations, and new, harder to achieve goals. Marie navigated this expertly, jumping through hoops for the new management, driving her team to higher and higher performance.

Marie wasn't just a terrific sales-woman she was also a good manager. She supported her team and insulated them frequently from the whims of upper management who would often distract them from performing and stress them out. At times she disagreed with her manager, but she always kept it professional. Colleagues marveled at how she could keep her cool in the face of so much pressure. Marie burned the midnight oil every night. She worked weekends. Her performance never dropped, and she consistently outperformed other regions. Eventually, she was running half of Canada.

One day, she got a call, it was her manager. They were *restructuring*. She bit her lip with irritation. After being with the company for years, Marie was unceremoniously laid off and replaced with someone who had no experience in a product category so complex but had "seniority" at the company.

Unfortunately, this type of story is all too commonplace today. I'm sure you can think of your own example of "Marie" in your workplace. Employees get fired for no reason all the time. But you might be wondering—what did Marie do wrong? What could she have possibly done to deserve this?

The only thing Marie ever did wrong was that she was always a 'Good Corporate Citizen.'

What is a Good Corporate Citizen?

A Good Corporate Citizen always puts the business first. The Good Corporate Citizen thinks it's his or her duty to identify problems and take them on—even if it means ignoring their own priorities to go and fix mistakes that aren't their responsibility, or problems that nobody else is seeing.

Good Corporate Citizens are the first to sign up for extracurricular activities. They're on all the committees. They volunteer for training they don't need. They are part of the company bowling league. (Hell, they may have even organized the bowling league in the first place.) Good Corporate Citizens are always trying to help the common good, but they don't do it because they're truly altruistic, they want visibility and brownie points.

In short, Good Corporate Citizens are not actively managing their careers, and they're not being honest with themselves. They are simply saying yes to all the things they think they're supposed to be saying yes to. But it's a façade. You aren't gaining any new skills by being at that meeting planning committee, and deep down, you know it. You're a Senior Analyst, and you want to be a meeting planner? Really? You want to order refreshments for the company picnic? That's not managing your career.

Let's take a look at Marie's strategy a little more closely. Like a lot of employees, Marie thought she had to put the needs of the business first. As a result, Marie ended up doing the 'right thing' to demonstrate her loyalty to the company. For instance, she always toed the company line and delivered messages to her team every time corporate asked her to, even when it didn't make a lot of sense. She was always up for a fool's errand. She allowed herself to get pulled into projects that helped her company but not her, and more often than not wound up donating her time and energy to lost causes. For instance, she helped a hopelessly struggling marketing team to develop new ideas and gave them advice on building materials, which took time away from her own goals and priorities.

Marie also wanted to be seen as "engaged," so she often participated in Women's Leadership summits, taking time away from executing. She would come home frustrated, as she didn't get much value out of the meetings. She sacrificed her reputation for the sake of the company. She used tactics to grow the business that the company demanded of her, but that hurt her personal credibility with customers she had important relationships with. (How could they trust her at a new company?) And worst of all, when the ship was going down, she believed her leaders when they said things would be fine.

Without meaning to, Marie's "Good Corporate Citizen" behavior consistently hurt her. The truth is, you can't take your managers at face value. Companies say they want employees to 'put the business first'—but in reality, putting the company first exposes you to a number of unexpected issues. Unless you're doing "selfish" things and playing the game, you will quickly find out that you are expendable.

Stability and Safety is a Myth

Does any of this sound familiar?

You've just been hired for a great new job, and you're negotiating the offer. The truth is, you're really excited about this position—it's everything you dreamed of—but you can't let them see that. The hiring manager tells you they are "taking a chance on you" and that your role is a "stretch." They say things like, the company is "making an investment," and they want a "long term commitment" from you. You find yourself agreeing with them. What choice do you have? You've been out of work for a few months, and you really need this job.

In truth, the company already knows your salary history, and they're just saying this to put you in a weaker negotiating position. They'll play hardball with set ranges for each job during negotiation, often bordering on outright deception. HR and hiring managers have one objective—keep compensation packages as low as possible.

As a result, you walk out of the negotiations feeling lucky you got the job, and you end up accepting a number that's less than you wanted— but not so demoralizing that you'd be willing to walk away from it.

You start your new job. Right away you develop a good rapport with your manager, after all, you have to live up to expectations. You get new projects and are presented with opportunities, and you redouble your efforts with every check-in. Meanwhile, you are trying to determine what it takes to get that elusive promotion they promised you during your interview. It all seems so impossible and completely subjective. You're never really sure where you stand or the exact criteria that your performance is being measured by.

Eventually, the company begins to struggle with performance, and finance groups start looking for places where they can save money to make their numbers. There's some office chatter going around about layoffs, but upper management calls an all-hands meeting and reassures the employees that everything will be fine. Nobody will get fired without plenty of warning and not without cause. But behind closed doors, management sits down and evaluates staffing levels and determines that certain departments need to be "right sized." Executive leadership agrees on a percentage staff cut for each department. Newer employees are laid off unexpectedly. They're completely blindsided because they thought they were in good standing this whole time. The company launches damage control, and once again, the employees are reassured. They're just doing a little 'housecleaning,' but the company is going to be fine.

You're faced with a dilemma. You've been getting great feedback from your manager, and you're busy with new projects, so you figure your job is safe, right? But employees are dropping like flies all around you, and your gut instinct is telling you to start looking for another job immediately.

The truth is, stability and safety are a myth. Companies groom employees to become "Good Corporate Citizens" because it serves them. And they will defend their interests at all costs, even if it means outright lying. They used to say that performance was your best friend, well those days are over. Your job is not a gift from others, and you can no longer sleepwalk through your career, hoping that everything will turn out okay. The only way to insure yourself in this type of environment is to stop doing what you think is right and start doing what is right for your career. In short, get more from your company than they get from you.

Individual Goals vs. Company Goals

You could go on LinkedIn right now and find a dozen garden variety of career articles with stock advice in them. They say things like, "Do more than you get paid for, and eventually, you will get paid more." Or ask your manager, "What keeps you up at night?"

That's exactly the type of shallow advice that is so pervasive because it's so easy. It's easy to go to a meeting and ask your boss what keeps them up at night. It looks like you're doing something important, but guess what—they can see through the b.s. You're just trying to look engaged.

When you have a selfish career, you have to invest more thoughtful effort into your career than that. It's not so easy. There's no panacea, no magic words you can say to your boss that will give you a successful career. You have to dig into where the problems are, and truly analyze every situation you find yourself in. You have to have real conversations with your leadership and develop real relationships with them. You have to read between the lines to understand what's actually critical to your bosses, instead of wasting your time on "check-box" projects. And you have to separate your individual goals from the goals of the company.

It isn't easy.

A few years ago, I found myself at an important crossroads. I was presented with two job offers at the same time. One job was doing the same exact thing I had always done: leading a portfolio of products. They were desperate to hire me to rehabilitate their brands and rebuild support for the sales force. I could also tell I would have to work 80 hours a week to accomplish this goal. Of course, they were offering significantly more compensation than the alternative option.

The alternative was a very different job, something I'd never done before. The role was enterprise-level within a marketing shared service organization. I wouldn't be attached to a business unit, I'd have no say in the direction we went in, and I wouldn't be able to make unilateral decisions. I'd always had roles where I knew that 'the buck stopped here.' This was different.

Even though it was less money, it was a different type of opportunity, and I knew I could get more out of it by learning new things. I would see a new part of my industry from the inside, which would expose me to new ways of working. This would allow me to focus on new experiences and gain skills that would be valuable to me in the future.

I took the second offer. I knew that the skills and experiences I gained would allow me to accomplish even more in the future, in my career as a whole. Part of my selfish strategy was focusing on my own goals of reaching my maximum potential and fitting this into the presented opportunities.

Company goals are set up to drive revenue and increase the overall profitability of the company. If you're not careful, company goals can distract you from what is in your best interest. Companies set goals in a formalized way, designed to ensure that employees place the company's needs above themselves. While this is a great method to ensure the success of the organization, it sacrifices individual development. At worst, blind alignment to these goals can cause you to sacrifice the achievement of what's best for you.

To combat this, you have to prioritize your goals, with little consideration of the company's needs or expected goals. You must go into your job knowing what experiences and development you want to accomplish for the year. Only then can you look at the needs of the company and determine how you can combine what you want to accomplish with what the company is trying to do.

When done thoughtfully, aligning your goals with the company's goals also forces a company to commit to your career development and skill building. And no one can take these away.

Broaden Your Skillset

After working on several different brands over my career, I started to recognize certain skill sets that were common among people in leadership positions. Most of these leaders weren't deep subject matter experts but were competent in a variety of subjects. They all had some sales and marketing experience, had spent some time in operations, had a strong financial background, and had developed big picture thinking. This allowed them to find new business opportunities that could help them grow the company through partnerships and acquisitions. I looked back on my career. Sure, I had roles that focused on operations, sales, brand strategy, and marketing—but I was missing some of the developmental experiences and skills I needed to get to the next level.

I took a look at the business unit I was working in. I saw there was room to increase the portfolio size through acquisitions, partnerships, or licensing deals. I decided to add this goal to my list and identify growth opportunities. This sparked discussions, and eventually, management agreed that I would work with a global strategy executive to evaluate the market opportunity of every potential deal we were considering. I learned so much just by adding this goal to my agenda. It also helped me to learn a variety of different businesses rapidly. I then took this knowledge and applied it at other companies with great success. It allowed me to build the foundation for my career and opened up promotion opportunities.

The goal setting process itself isn't complicated. Hold a personal off-site meeting for a day where you can take a step back from distractions and focus on where you are today in your career, and where you want to be.
Outline the specific skills or experiences you want to build over the course of the year. Work hard to focus on developing specific competencies that can never be taken away. Once you establish your goals, develop an understanding of the company's goals, and start to apply them to your own.

Identify key initiatives and projects or tasks that align with the company's goals but also allow you to develop new skills. A key insight is to make sure you learn a variety of foundational skills you can build on over time into advanced competencies. While the hope is that the new skills you are developing are valued by your current company, do a broader evaluation of the skills that would set you apart from your peers in your industry as a whole. You want the skills you are developing to be even more valuable to you than they are to your current employer.

Develop a "Trade-Off" Mentality

To ensure you are getting more out of your company than they are getting out of you, in addition to goal setting and skill development, you have to consider the trade-off between three factors at any given time. The three factors are: compensation, effort, and experiences.

In other words, you have to think of what you're getting versus what you're giving at all times. It is critical to develop a trade-off mentality using these three factors. If you can't develop a comfort level with the trade-offs between those three, your company will get more out of you than you are getting out of them.

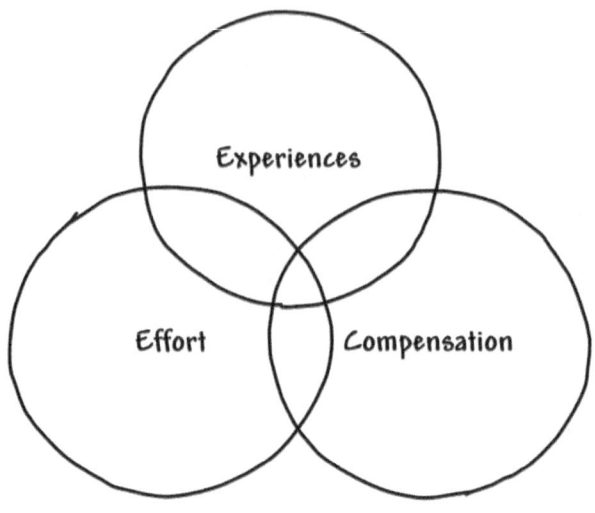

The choices are simple. If you are confronted with a situation where you are paid less than you are worth, you must either give less effort or learn new skills that will benefit you. If you're getting great experiences that will build your skill set and you can take those skills anywhere, it is justifiable to take less than the maximum amount of money you could make elsewhere. In this situation, it would be worth the effort. If it requires significant effort, but you aren't learning anything new, you would want to be highly paid for your services. Last, if you are not gaining new experiences and you are not being compensated fairly, give the minimal amount of effort to successfully complete your job. Typically, if a company is paying you under your market value, they're not likely to reward or even recognize a high level of performance anyway.

This last strategy is hard for a lot of people to implement. Most people fear that their performance won't be high enough, someone will find out, and they will be laid off. This isn't the case. Layoffs and terminations rarely happen because of actual performance issues but rather because the employees are not focused on the subjective factors that are most likely to drive success in an organization. Let Marie's story be a warning to us all, if you are too focused on being a Good Corporate Citizen, you could find yourself without a corporation to work for at all.

TAKE HOME LESSONS:
- Company goal-setting places the organization's needs first and minimizes your professional development that would guarantee your success over the long-term.
- Establishing the skills and experiences you want to develop before company goal-setting is a key step in you getting more out of your company than they get out of you.
- After determining your goals, identify projects or initiatives you can use to develop new skills. This will result in the commitment of the company and manager to your development.
- Commit yourself to making sure you get more out of your company than they get out of you. Manage this through routine tradeoffs between monetary compensation: experiences: effort. Generally, you are able to satisfy two of the three dimensions at any one time.

ACTION ITEM: Match the skills from the chapter take-homes to a project that you can complete in alignment with company goals. Determine whether you should formalize this, or where you keep it information and 'just do it.'

CHAPTER II
DON'T BE A CORPORATE DRONE, YOUR CAREER IS A COMPLEX GAME YOU HAVE TO PLAY

When I took over the team, I could tell that Elle had potential. She was young, but it was obvious that she could analyze problems and come up with solutions very quickly and easily. She worked hard, but the problem was she was working on projects way below what she was fully capable of, minimizing her contributions and visibility.

For months I watched Elle as she managed "checkbox" projects and did lower level work for others, rather than focusing on projects that would add significant value to the organization. For instance, she would chase down stakeholders for feedback on document edits for others. Another time she pulled together and completed internal communication documents that had little value. She did all this without question or complaint, but clearly not exhibiting any excitement about her work.

Elle would take whatever work came her way, no matter what it was, just to stay busy. As a result, she was buried with busier work.

One day I asked Elle to sit down and have coffee with me. As we talked, it was obvious she wanted more from her career. She wanted to learn, she was in the middle of pursuing her Master's degree. She wanted to contribute, and she wanted to advance. She confided to me that every day she'd gone home from work frustrated. Her face got flush when she said it, wondering if I was going to get angry. She knew she wasn't gaining any momentum, but she couldn't figure out why.

The reason was simple—it was all because she wasn't playing "the game." She had become a Corporate Drone and didn't even know it.

What is a Corporate Drone?

A Corporate Drone is someone who is just surviving.

While Good Corporate Citizens will stand up for what's 'right' and what's 'best' for the company, drones don't make waves. They go in and do their jobs, but they are not actively managing their interactions. It's as if they're sleepwalking through their careers. They aren't thinking proactively about meetings, creating strategies, or setting themselves up for success. In other words, they aren't "playing the game."

You may survive as a corporate drone—I've known some that have lasted for eons—but that's not what this book is about. If you are cool with having the same job for years, and never getting any momentum or steam, then this book isn't for you.

As I said in the last chapter, the solutions I present in this book aren't "magic pills" or panaceas. It requires work, with the emphasis on being proactive rather than passive. The first conscious step you must take in prioritizing yourself is making the decision: I won't be a drone any longer!

Drones don't differentiate themselves from others, and as a result, they most often wind up in dead-end careers. They are very good at going through the motions, doing their jobs just like everybody else, collecting annual 2.5% raises, and often rely on others to manage their career. For instance, they are always waiting for someone to give them an opportunity to advance, rather than actively owning and managing their own career. They don't stand out, and it's often because they don't have the roadmap so they can.

A lot of drones are very talented at their jobs. The problem isn't lack of talent, it's that they don't know that they're playing a game. Because they've never been coached or given winning strategies to use, they don't know how to manage their careers. Surviving is more important to them than the perception others have of them. They don't own their personal brand. As a result, they get demoralized and eventually turn into drones.

Don't worry if you are reading this and have come to the shocking realization that you are a corporate drone. Once a corporate drone realizes they're playing a game and a change needs to happen, they can immediately start to think strategically about how to navigate and win.

I told Elle I would help her. I started to give her the rules of the game and some hints about how to navigate the game board. I compared it to playing the classic game Risk. Similar to Risk, advancing in a corporation requires diplomacy. No matter how much you try, it will also involve conflict and thinking several moves ahead, but when played correctly results in conquest.

What winning looks like can be very different for different people, though. For some, it's a promotion, for others it's more freedom within their role, and for others, it's leaving when you're presented with a better opportunity.

So what happened to Elle? Well, she immediately started seeking out projects that were worth her time. She prioritized herself, not the company. And she strategically avoided projects that didn't match her greatest strengths, interests, or the skillsets she wanted to build. Her mindset changed, and she learned how to maximize her strengths and not sign up for things that played to her weaknesses or weren't in her best interest.

This new mindset allowed her to shift from being bogged down in the day-to-day details of her job, and begin focusing on the future of her career and making sure that she was on track towards her goals. I started encouraging her to perform above what her title was, which made her not only perform better but want to do better in her career overall.

Next, Elle began to create projects on her own to solve problems. She demonstrated how the work she was doing would reflect positively on her boss and team. She presented her ideas on how to fit these projects into the overall company strategy, and they were well received and often implemented. She gave a presentation to 200 people in her department, and people told her 'it was just like listening to a TED talk.'

Elle stopped caring more about the company than herself and her ambitions. She learned not to invest too much into any one thing, her company, or her boss. She developed relationships with a key outside partners to learn as much as should could and extend her professional network.

She started focusing on how she was curating her future rather than passively coasting through her career. She outlined her goals and made sure the day to day activities didn't bog her down and distract her. She became more objective about each situation she encountered and was able to always remind herself that she was the only person that had her best interests in mind. Within the course of a year, she collected experiences that set in motion a promotion but simultaneously resulted in an opportunity to hop to another company for an expanded role and a salary that was so much higher it was personally game-changing. Frankly, I was stunned. I never expected it. I figured I'd be able to expand her role and give her more, but I couldn't. She was no longer a corporate drone.

The point is—your career is a complex game you have to play.

So, are you the type that is OK with just coasting by and letting others dictate the course of your career? Or are you in it to win it?

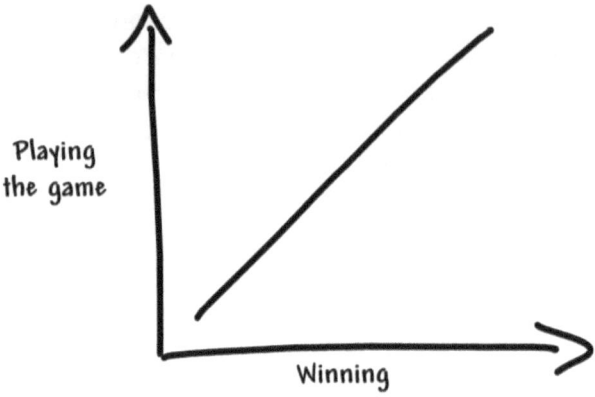

Winning the Game

The concept of 'play the game' might be the easiest to understand but the hardest to implement. It's very hard to admit you are a cog in a wheel, a small piece of a huge puzzle, or a background actor in a movie or play. You are replaceable at any time, and shockingly, you can be replaced easily. Acknowledging that it's a game, and your place in the grand scheme of things gives you the objectivity you need to gauge whether what you are doing is working for you, or against you.

Unfortunately, if you are working for a company that is larger than 1,000 people, you usually have a smaller impact on the overall success or failure of the company, then you think you do. Playing the game means knowing that you are not the most important person in the company. This helps insulate you from bad things happening, but it also gives you the ability to prioritize yourself above the company and others.

But shouldn't we all do what's best for the company? Doing what's best for the company is the right thing to do when it aligns with what is best for you, but if it conflicts with what is best for you, then be wary. This game has winners and losers. It's not a level playing field, and no one is working in your best interests other than you (and in most cases…you aren't working in your best interests either).

More times than not, when confronted with a situation where you have to 'do what's best for the company' there is a high likelihood you are usually 'doing what's <u>worst</u> for you.'

Any tasks or projects that force you to ignore your own goals and distract you from them is what I'm talking about. Examples include:
- Projects that come about because someone else didn't do their work properly and you could fix it
- Projects arising from when someone forgot to do something entirely
- Projects that pop up when you identify a problem no one has even thought of

- Activities involving coaching someone or contributing to another's success that is a peer or when they aren't your direct report, or you are a formal mentor

These projects are usually low value and help others more than they benefit you. Many people would argue that they are doing these things so they will be viewed as being a "team player" or that they're playing the hero and saving the company from major issues. In my experience, I've not found that to be the case. Typically, they are micro-issues. Someone else was responsible for doing them correctly the first time. If someone else has ignored their responsibilities or is incapable of doing them, why would you bail them out at your own expense? And why would you hide them from the company so they are just swept under the rug, never to be addressed?

I'm not suggesting you ignore a glaring problem, particularly if there is a chance others will know you were aware of it and didn't alert anyone. I'm suggesting instead to ensure the issue is raised and the person responsible for it corrects it versus 'chipping in' and getting no credit for being 'the fixer.' Even if you do get credit for it, these projects aren't usually career makers. They are usually things where leadership says, "Why did it go wrong in the first place?" In other words, let the drones do it.

I've seen a number of 'fixers' in my career, and typically they languish at the same level because they are perceived as having a limited skill set, aren't strategic thinkers, and toil away 60 hours a week solving problems that other people created—only to get a new assignment and start over again. It's a never-ending cycle for them and usually gets worse over time. 'Fixers' get increasingly tougher problems over time, resulting in projects that at some point, turn into unsolvable situations where you eventually fail. It's reactive in nature, and not the proactive approach that helps you maximize your career. As your reputation builds as the 'fixer,' it binds you to one company and often a small set of leaders who make use of it. The 'fixer' can't port their skills to other organizations because being the 'fixer' has more to do with subjective factors such as reputation and grit than it does skills that are valuable anywhere.

Drones, 'heroes' and 'fixers' are in a disadvantageous position because they are always under intense pressure to fix something that is badly broken, rather than taking something good and making it great.

Be a People Appeaser

Drones are expendable, but your relationships with people may save you. But for that plan to work you better 'play the game.'

A key to 'playing the game' is appeasing your internal customers and colleagues. It's actually very simple. People want to work with people they get along with. Telling them what they want to hear is surprisingly effective and rarely comes back to haunt you the way being the bearer of uncomfortable truths does.

For much of my career, I've felt the need to tell executives 'what's really going on with the company.' I thought the transparency was helping the company, and I was doing the right thing. One time, after a manager's meeting, I told our GM that we needed a "ground up approach because what existed currently wasn't nearly equipped to do the job effectively." I meant it as constructive criticism, but it completely backfired!

He had created this state of things, so he immediately snapped, "If that's your opinion, then you don't have what it takes to lead this." I had to avoid that guy for about three months until he was 'given a new opportunity' at the company, and a new leader took his place.

Not only does this truth-telling backfire almost 100% of the time, it's akin to calling the baby 'ugly.' Executives, especially those that had a hand in building the company, are going to naturally have an extremely closeminded approach to hearing new information. They don't see the flaws in their work, they see only the positives, and they don't want to admit their mistakes. It's too risky for them. When someone tells them there is more work to be done, or that they missed something in the process, it will be interpreted as unsolicited criticism.

This puts them on the defensive and places you in a position where you are viewed as a threat. If your effort is to cultivate supporters of your career, or at least ensure others have a neutral opinion rather than a negative one, making yourself a threat isn't going to help you. Better to cultivate a relationship with them and acknowledge the good you see. Resist the urge to critique the situation but rather offer alternatives for how the company could take something good and make it even better.

If confronted with someone who is pushing you to give constructive criticism, be cautious. Avoid debate on true and glaring deficiencies. Often you will offend the responsible party or even worse, become part of the party who is tasked with fixing the problem, once again...distracting you from accomplishing your goals. Don't be afraid to punt the discussion to a later time. Say something like, "I'd love to collect my thoughts and give you a thoughtful answer," so you don't end up saying something you can't take back.

Solve Your Manager's Problems

Playing the game with your manager (and your manager's manager) is critical to your success. It starts with being a resource to them and ends with reminding them what that resource has done for them, sandwiched by aligning on goals that are important to you both.

This requires you to understand your manager's priorities and challenges. These problems will usually be higher level, more strategic, and more valuable than the task-oriented projects you could get if they are assigning them. When you learn what those things are, take a step back, be open to the opportunities and growth that could be had through solving those problems. Create recommendations and a plan to solve those problems and present them to your manager.

Remember not to let your manager's boss's priorities supersede your real manager's. It's tempting to fall into the ego trap of being tapped for a project by your boss's boss. If you aren't making sure your direct manager's priorities come first, it can be threatening and can put you in a bad position with your manager. If there was a percentage of focus to apply, I would say 90% direct manager service and 10% manager's manager service. In nearly all circumstances, your manager will need the approval of his manager to promote you or give you key projects. The 10% rule will give them enough info to be supportive of you without making your direct manager feel like you don't care enough about them.

Play Well with Others

It's important to take a different approach with your external customers. You should tell them what they *need* to hear, rather than what they want to hear. This is because customers or vendors you work with may be able to help you advance your career more than your company, manager, or work colleagues could.

The company you work for doesn't have an incentive to see you explore other opportunities, and neither does your manager or colleagues. For instance, I've had colleagues talk me out of looking outside because it would have made their job harder or less stable if I had left.

There's an incredible amount of success you can achieve if you work with your external customers and partners, if you are transparent with them, and explain your company goals to them. At a minimum, they will want you to succeed because it ensures they will have a long and successful collaboration with you and your company. Resist the urge to hide these goals, and take time to explain them on all levels: corporate, business unity, department, and initiative level. Tying these things together is even more powerful and can result in a more productive relationship.

Playing the game with external companies when you are casually or actively looking for new job opportunities is critically important. I can't stress this enough. Tell them what they want to hear both about you and about how you see their company or potential roles. No matter how much people complain about the companies they work for, I've found they are very protective of their company to outsiders. It's tribalism coming through. When you are networking, or in discussions with any representative of a company, you have to remain positive about what you can provide and resist the urge to criticize their current processes. The best thing to do is reinforce the value you can bring, the service you can provide, and how you can help them succeed.

TAKE HOME LESSONS
- Fundamental to everything is: you must 'play the game.' This requires constant effort and diligence but ensures you are not putting too much effort into the priorities of others and can keep focused on separating the company's activities and priorities from your own.
- Doing what is best for the company and sacrificing your own priorities results in distracting you from both short-term and long-term success.
- Playing the game with your internal customers or colleagues means being amicable, getting along, telling them what they want to hear, and keeping everyone on your good side. Most people aren't self-aware enough to accept criticisms no matter how constructive your intent may be.
- Playing the game with your manager means aligning your activities to their challenges, but with an eye towards developing the skills that will be beneficial to you. Focus on service to them and reinforce what you are bringing consistently.
- Playing the game with your external vendors, customers, or partners can align their goals to yours and result in better work product. The financial viability of your external partners is worth paying for, and extreme focus on cost savings will usually result in less quality, service, or relationships.
- Playing the game with other companies means telling them what they want to hear

about you. This includes being positive about the company and people there, wanting to help them succeed, wanting to stay there a long time, and not highlighting you are overly interested in development or promotions.

ACTION ITEM: Ask your boss the next time you see him/her what their greatest challenge is. Tell him/her you want to talk about how you can help them solve that problem or at least make it better. Try to understand what your boss's challenge is. What's important to them? Ask them in a way that doesn't sound contrived; so they have to be much more expansive. Stock questions like, "What keeps you up at night?" will only get you stock crappy one-word answers. Ask open-ended questions. For instance, "What problems have you been unable to solve, and why?"

CHAPTER III
DON'T GET DISTRACTED BY PROMOTIONS, BUILD SKILLS INSTEAD

"Aren't you worried? What are you gonna' do?"

Thirty minutes after I got laid off, I was sitting down to a celebratory lunch with my direct reports and a variety of other colleagues I had worked with for the past four years. They were more worried than I was.

"There are hardly any places to work in Pittsburgh, and there definitely aren't very many that pay well...."
"Are you worried about finding a new job?" "You have to send Jackson to college, I can't believe you're not more worried-- you look like you don't even care!" In fact, I could barely contain my smile.

They talked about how panicked they would be if they were laid off suddenly, and how stressful it would be to look for a job and be faced with the unknown. What they didn't know was that I had built my career with a focus on experiences, skills, and learnings that were extremely valuable and unique. At 8 AM the next morning, I was making calls and reaching out to a variety of contacts I had made over my career to let them know I was available for consulting. The next four months, while I wasn't working at a full-time job, I had consulting projects lined up and was generating revenue through my LLC.

I was able to do this because of the broad set of skills I had built over my career, because I had experience in many different markets, and because I had created frameworks and processes that could be applied anywhere.

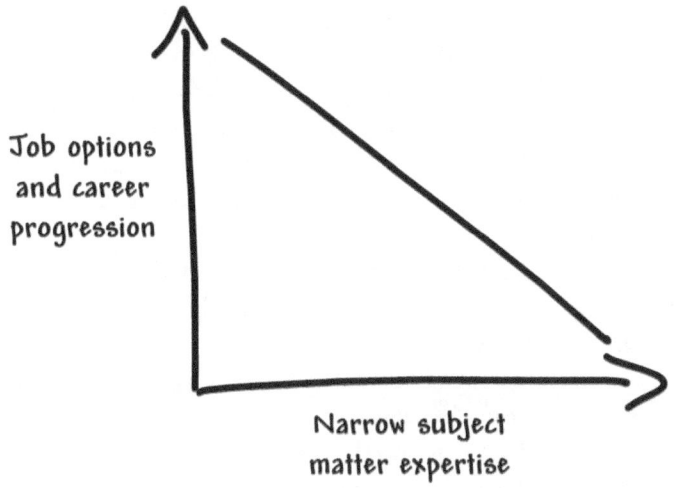

My approach is different than most people's because generally, people are focused only on getting promotions at the expense of everything else. They unwittingly continue to develop narrower and narrower skill sets that actually reduce the number of skills they have over time, rather than increasing them. Yes, they may get promotions, but they also often end up specific subject matter experts. They know a lot about a small number of topics, at a very deep level. And this makes it more difficult for them to find jobs quickly that match their specific expertise and will pay them the highest amount possible. It does nothing to protect them against layoffs.

What I recommend in this chapter, and book overall, will give you the greatest opportunity for growth over the long term, and increase your overall value. This should help you find a new role more easily should something unexpected happen, like if your company suddenly downsizes. This strategy will help insulate you from office politics and make sure you can find a job anywhere at any time. It will also allow you to have more control over your day-to-day job activities because you won't be so fearful about losing your current role. You won't operate from a place of fear and risk avoidance. And you can walk away from your employer at any time with the confidence to create a consultancy that you can build into a full-time business, or make money off of while you look for another full-time role if that is your preference. And the added bonus is...you will still get the promotions, but it will be on your terms rather than your employer's.

To put this strategy into motion, though, you'll have to shift your thinking away from chasing the next promotion, and towards building valuable skills.

Resist the Urge (Why you shouldn't take an Easy Promotion)

I used to chase promotions. I wasn't thoughtful or carefully thinking about each situation, I just wanted the better title and the money.

For instance, early in my career, I went from being a Group Manager to Director, but to get it I had to take over two old products and responsibility for an acquired business that had gone hopelessly sideways. It was an unfixable situation; the business was only going down. If I had been more thoughtful and asked myself, "Is this the right role for me? Will I be learning more? Or am I just chasing the money and a fancy title?" I could have avoided this mess.

In today's corporate environment, after three or four years in any business, you have to move on. You have to take your tricks-- which no longer work-- to a new place and start fresh. You cannot do this if you are chasing promotions.

I won't pretend to tell you this is easy. You must be much more focused on road-mapping the skills and experiences you want, and making sure you're able to achieve them, and not get tempted by the offer of an easy upward ascension. You also have to personally resist the urge to focus on advancing within a company in the same role you have had previously.

When I've brought up this concept with others, the conversation very often leads to their desire to get promoted and make more money. They ask me, "Why shouldn't I be trying for the next promotion? It's the only way I'm going to make more money and get the title I deserve."

Yes, I recognize promotions are important. And it certainly is one way to make more money and get increased recognition. But I also recognize I've had promotions that happened so quickly, I wasn't focused on whether it was the right role at the right time. I just wanted the advancement and the extra money. I can also look back and recognize there were certain promotions where I was taking on a role that was not going to set me up for success. I have experienced both these situations, and after I was promoted, I found myself trying to fix something unfixable. My time in those roles didn't teach me anything new, and instead, it required me to use the skills I already had to try and save a sinking ship. The problem was, no amount of effort was going to fix the problems. I had promoted myself right into a dead end.

To avoid this trap, you can employ what I call "Three Strategies to Avoid a "Dead End Job."

Be an "All-Terrain" Employee

The first strategy is to focus on a wide variety of experiences and making sure you're doing lots of different things. Like an all-terrain vehicle that's able to handle many types of surfaces, with this strategy, the goal is on gaining as many broad experiences as possible. This means you must expose yourself to different business challenges in different environments.

Colleagues I have been impressed by the most--in the quality of their work, the quality of their solutions and ideas, and their apparent ability to accomplish their job easily and successfully-- all had a background built on a wide variety of experiences. They worked in different types of businesses both during good times and bad and have 'seen it all.' They were "All-Terrain" employees.

The key is to make sure there are a variety of business challenges you are helping to solve and that you are experiencing different market conditions. This may mean gaining experiences in a highly competitive environment as well as an innovator environment with limited competition. It could also include working on a business that is a commodity and then transitioning to a business focused on building a brand. It's important to work at both the enterprise-level and within a business unit that is driving sales.

Let me give you an example of someone I worked with, who really embodied this strategy and used it to her advantage.

When Leah first started, she had just finished her MBA after a number of years of being a very successful saleswoman. She'd always wanted to do marketing, so she jumped at a chance to take this role as a product and marketing manager. Unfortunately, the leader she was reporting to focused her on creating sales materials and doing grunt work, like general sales support. Leah did great work, but she felt boxed in and disconnected from her overall career strategy.

After about two years, her boss left, and she was transferred over to me. During our first few meetings, Leah asked me right away, "What projects do I need to take on so I can get promoted?" She let me know she had no issue with working hard, but she wanted to make sure she was advancing. After all, she'd had to sacrifice a lot of hobbies and personal time for this job.

So, I took a deeper look into what skills Leah had. After a few months, we finally had the conversation she'd been waiting for, but it wasn't what she expected. I said, "We don't want to approach this by loading you up with random projects. Whether it's getting you to the next level or not, you need to work on skill building and experience, rather than making it about promotions." I explained that she had to approach this with an eye to the long term.

Leah was interested, so we mapped out the hard and soft skills. Among other things, they included some new areas for her, such as building business plans, developing a better approach to keynote presentations, and running advisory meetings. We expanded her range of environments to test out her new skills. So what happened? She did all the work she was asked to do, and she did it with a great attitude. She even completed it all faster than expected. I put in for her promotion, but it was kicked back because all promotions were frozen due to the company's financial underperformance. Making it even worse for her, I left the company soon after and the new leadership kept moving the goalposts on her. She was stuck at the same level.

But Leah's story has a happy ending. After the company proved to her that they weren't going to promote her, and she got tired of the broken promises and bad attitudes, she jumped to another company. It was lateral, but she got herself into a position where she could make a greater impact. And because she had focused on experiencing many different "terrains" and developing new skills-- instead of chasing promotions-- she's been designated a high performer by her boss. Most importantly, she's delivering this high performance with very little stress and working minimal office hours because of the skills she worked so hard to develop. She's now able to do more volunteering and equestrian competitions, which are her real loves.

Develop a "Swiss ARMY" Skillset

The reality is in-line, or "easy," promotions usually require you to focus even more on developing and advancing skills you already have rather than learning new skills. Unless your promotion or advancement is going to give you opportunities to leverage the foundational skills you have and apply them in different ways, you are at risk of becoming a subject matter expert. You'll just be sharpening the one knife that you already have, rather than adding new knives that can solve other problems.

We need a Swiss ARMY skill set nowadays.

While it may appear getting promotions is the only way to build your career and get ahead, it may put you at risk, because the skills you develop could be too specific to the company you're working for. It's very important not to become an expert at any one specific skill. Becoming an expert in that specific skill encourages management and leadership to continue to exploit that skill for an indefinite period. It will prevent you from learning and having the broad experiences you need. It will also often result in developing skills which work for just one industry or market condition rather than learning a framework that you can adjust to any type of product, during any business cycle, in any industry. Instead, work on developing broad skill sets that you can apply to anything.

No one can take away experiences or skills from you once you have them. Just like a Swiss ARMY knife or other multi-tools, you can use them for a lifetime as long as you keep them free from rust-- aka. continue exercising the skills you have developed.

Create Frameworks and Process Maps (for the road)

Many people create spectacular ways to approach problems and then forget they created them in the first place, or didn't save them and have to recreate it from the ground up over and over again. Make sure, throughout the project you're working on, you're saving these frameworks and process maps for your own future use. Make sure you have transferred this knowledge from the company to your own personal files so you can use them in a new role at a new company, or when addressing problems as a consultant. Also, make sure you do not take any confidential information as this can put you at risk of losing your job.

Don't underestimate the usability of even small project frameworks, some of these are the most useful because they can be applied to routine projects to make them more efficient. For instance, if you created an amazing Xcel spreadsheet that helped shave thousands off the company's bottom line, or you put together a handy template for writing short video scripts-- make sure you transfer those over to your personal computer for later use.

As you work through these new experiences, building skills, and understanding different market situations, you'll want to develop processes and frameworks you can use anywhere and in any situation. Take these experiences and combine similar ones together to create frameworks and process maps for future use. When you've validated that the frameworks will work across a variety of situations, and you can fill them in when facing different market challenges, anytime you need them.

In conclusion, while the skills and experiences you gain are very important, being able to speak to the experiences is also critical. If you can't convince others that you can take these skills and apply them to different challenges a business may face, then they are basically useless. So, rack up experiences that you can talk about with others. Try to think through how you would present the case to them by developing concise explanations of what the business challenge was, what skills you used to solve the problem, and the ultimate result.

And when you are pushing your managers to give you new opportunities and broaden your horizons, you want to make sure you're also talking about solving problems that are important to the corporation, to your manager, and also to you. If you're solving challenges your manager is facing, this will allow them to relax and increase your role to be much broader than your actual job description.

Remember, this is a skill aggregation game. Most people are waiting for their boss to tell them what skills to develop, and most people don't know what skills to combine to make themselves very unique. So, instead of thinking, "What do I need to get promoted?" Focus instead of what will make you unique, the most well rounded, and the most experienced.

TAKE HOME LESSONS:
- Focusing on experiences and skill building will help you more in the long run than focusing on inline promotions, which can make your skillset more and more narrow. It

also insulates you from fear of losing your job and allows you to be more in demand if you wanted to leave or are unexpectedly downsized.
- Focus on creating a diverse background of experiences and skills rather than becoming a subject matter expert. Resist the urge to become an expert at any one thing unless you have already laid the foundation of a broad skill set.
- Push managers to give you opportunities that are outside the norm. Rack up experiences you can speak to with others that depict the challenges you have faced and the value you bring.
- Be an "All-Terrain" employee. Work to experience different market situations, different business models, and different types of products like brands and commodities.
- Create repeatable processes and frameworks from your experiences. Write them down and keep in your personal files so you have a library of frameworks you can lean on to make future projects easier and to prevent you from having to 'reinvent the wheel.'
- No one can take experiences and skills away from you once you have them. If you think creatively, you can make your job easier by using them and can even use them in a consulting capacity.

ACTION ITEM: Remove yourself from work and identify two skills you want to learn this year or the two experiences that will be valuable to you and different than what a normal employee would do.

CHAPTER IV
NEVER SHARE YOUR TRUE FEELINGS OR ULTIMATE AGENDA

"We're going in a different direction and bringing in someone else to run North America," my boss said, nervously. "You were promoted about a year ago, and we feel you are in the right spot."

I was in shock. I didn't see this coming at all. After it sunk in, I couldn't see straight.

Over the three years I'd been at this company I'd led the growth of an ancient product by over 65%, coached and mentored a large team of high performing marketers, turned around a dog product resulting in its first unit growth in years, and worked tirelessly to rehabilitate an infamous pharmaceutical brand after an unprecedented public relations nightmare. I had been promoted twice in that time and continued to get consistent positive feedback in my role both verbally and with multiple exceed ratings on annual reviews I had worked hard and consistently expressed how much I wanted to be at the company to help it grow, which I was uniquely positioned to do.

Now they picked someone from another country to do the job I was perfect for? Someone who had no experience in the US market. I kept thinking, *they didn't even give me a chance to make my case.*

"I just want an opportunity to continue growing in my role, add more value, make more money," I said. Even as I said it, I realized it sounded lame. I felt the ground slipping away under my feet.

He sat back in his seat and replied, "If advancement is what is important to you, this probably isn't the right place for you. And you already make too much money...so I'd be happy for what you are getting now."

Shocked, I blurted out, "I've never heard of a company that doesn't want people to push themselves. It's a dog eat dog environment here that everyone encourages. And how can you say I make too much money when the executive team is pulling down tens of millions each year? Those decisions aren't sixty times better than the decisions I or anyone else at my level makes."

The meeting didn't get better from there...

Within two months of this conversation, I was pulled into a room and told there was reorganization happening. I was being laid off.

Looking back, I can trace these surprising events to two or three interactions...and in each of those interactions I made the mistake of sharing my true feelings. True feelings about my role. True feelings about concerns I had in the company's direction and risks that I saw. True feelings about how it was obvious they didn't want to hear my true feelings.

The fact of the matter is work is not the place to share your true feelings. Not with anyone. No matter how good your intentions. One way or another, your words will always come back to bite you in the ass.

Words can hurt you.

Oh, when you share too much with others, it's such a slippery slope. The worst part about it is finding out that people you thought you could trust, people you thought were your friends, will burn you. Nothing is worse than losing trust in people that you thought had your back.

Without even meaning to, the people you work with-- coworkers, bosses, peers, your boss's boss-- will use your words against you. Whether it's tattling on you, undermining your career, or just plain gossip, there are consequences for oversharing. Someone could take advantage of you once they know your secret weaknesses (which you gladly volunteered to them). Someone could tell the boss how you feel about them and ruin your relationship forever. You risk losing credibility and being unable to get buy-in from your team because you got too familiar with them. A jealous rival could undermine you by telling leadership you aren't a team player, and you get parked in a job with no hopes of moving forward or shifted over to something painful that sets you up for failure. Believe me…it happens, and I've seen it way more than once.

This book is about making sure you have choices and can navigate your career at your own pace, taking your chosen path, not the path of others. When you share too much, there is a real risk of someone taking control of your path. And if you confront this "traitor" publically, then your career at that company is done.

Obviously, you should keep your feelings close to your vest. But it's only one piece of the strategy.

While there are a lot of things you shouldn't, share, you shouldn't stop yourself from maximizing huge opportunities for action and advancement. If you've done many of the things in this book, and you have carefully understood what your boss's challenges are, and you're delivering on those-- there is a place for you to start calling in favors, spreading influence, and making things more advantageous for you. When these conversations are entered thoughtfully and strategically, and you are in control of everything that comes out of your mouth, you can easily activate others on your behalf, to advance your career.

I call this technique 'Activating your Advocates.'

Activate Your Advocates

Activating others through conversations takes planning and foresight, a little bit like playing chess. You need to think a few moves ahead at all times. Remember those Corporate Drones I spoke about in the last chapter? Lucky for you, most people are drones. They aren't good at playing "career chess," they aren't thinking ahead, and they're most likely sleepwalking through their career. These people can be activated on your behalf. Even leaders.

Now, I'm not saying you should abjectly manipulate people. Over time, people will figure that out, and it will burn you. However, developing relationships with people is key and is the foundation and groundwork needed for you to activate others. Without it, no matter how hard you try, it won't happen. Build your relationships on common thoughts and opinions that you share with others. Likeminded people tend to feel that they're "in the fight together" and this isn't a bad thing.

Your aim here is to create advocates and evangelists for you and for your ideas. Remember that your ideas are your power. When others adopt them, your influence goes through the roof. And when your advocates start sharing your ideas with extended colleagues, you'll know you've truly specially activated them.

Once you've developed these relationships, you can begin activating others by consistently seeding your ideas into the conversation. Never ask people to do anything on your behalf directly, but rather appeal to their logic or emotions. Revisit the subject routinely, bring it up over and over with new examples of how your idea could be tested and proven. Develop catch phrases that describe your ideas in a way that is easy to remember. And offer people payoffs at the end, if they've successfully helped you in your mission.

You are looking to nudge others into action. You have to show them how the action is going to pay off personally for them. If necessary, play into people's laziness. We are all lazy, to some degree. Most people want to take the well-worn road or the path that looks easiest and safe. You can invite people to become advocates for your ideas by selling it to them as something that will result in less hassle for them over the long run or solves an immediate problem. This is often the easiest way to activate your boss or other leaders in the organization.

To sum it up, the process of activating people looks like this: 1) develop a strong relationship; 2) seed ideas; 3) repetition); 4) use catch phrases; 5) give them a payoff.

Once you have internalized this technique, you can begin using it in the most dangerous territory of all-- check-ins and performance reviews.

Learn to Navigate Check-Ins and Performance Reviews

There are a variety of situations where sharing your true feelings is particularly dangerous, these include performance check-ins and reviews. If you don't carefully consider what you are saying during these situations and guard against sharing your true feelings, it can make you look like a complainer, or an employee whose difficult to get along with and doesn't fit in. This can put you at risk of being passed over for promotion or even being laid off.

These are very formal conversations and should be treated as such. You want to make sure you're controlling the meeting as best you can, by going in with an agenda. Many people get lulled into thinking that their boss is their friend. They aren't.

Go in with a plan for action and activity-- don't be that passive person without a plan. Develop an agenda going in, and with the intention of reinforcing your point of view and creating advocates for that point of view. Most people go in with no plan and end up reacting to what others say and just talk and talk without stopping to listen. They are waiting to react rather than listening so they can respond.

Let me give you an example. I had a conversation with my boss to discuss my career. What I was trying to do was get him to advocate on my behalf for a promotion. He started talking about potentially moving me to a group of people I wasn't super excited to work with, and where I wouldn't be learning anything new.

I wanted him to know I was willing to change positions if it was an improvement for me, but I didn't want to make a lateral move. I waited for him to finish what he was saying and then I said something to the effect of, "Look I'm not trying to run away from a job. I like my job. I like working with you. And I like these things too much to move if it isn't for a promotion."

I leveraged my strong relationship with him to lay the groundwork to ask for what I wanted. I seeded the idea by repeatedly telling him I liked my job but was looking for a promotion. It made him feel good to advocate for my advancement. And I also gave him a payoff. After all, he needs to look like he's promoting people under him as well. Now he can move me up the ladder, where he'll have another key ally in another part of the organization, and leverage someone else into the role I will soon be vacating.

Back It Up with Facts

Guaranteed, at some point in your career, you will be asked the million-dollar question, "So, how do you like your job?"

My advice is, don't take the bait.

Leadership will always be trying to gauge your level of satisfaction with your current role in the company. A big part of controlling the conversation during performance check-ins is not letting yourself be lowballed into sharing your true feelings about a variety of subjects, that includes your feelings about your job.

Sharing your true feelings about your job can lead to skepticism about your commitment to the company or to the role, and can make your manager second guess you being on their team, and them supporting your career. The reality is that most managers aren't really good ones. I've had only two truly great ones in my career, and you can't leave your career plans in the hands of a person who in all likelihood is mediocre at best.

So, stick to the facts.

The greatest way to tell whether or not you're sharing something you shouldn't is whether or not it is objective or subjective. What this means is, it's fine to share something that is objectively true or false, if it's factual or it speaks to the truth, or it speaks to a specific timeline of events. What you want to steer clear of is sharing emotions about a situation, feelings about an event (or a person), and anything else that can't be backed up by facts.

Other dangerous topics include being asked for feedback or feelings about peers, your boss, or your feelings about other leaders. There's a very basic rule of thumb I like to follow in these types of situations, just remember, "Snitches get Stitches."

Snitches Get Stitches

It is impossible to know where anyone's true loyalties lie. There may be relationships you are unaware of that can result in a conversation you *thought* was confidential being shared with someone unexpectedly. People can't help themselves. In fact, even I can admit I'm guilty of doing this when I knew it would help me out personally. When this happens, it is impossible to put the genie back in the bottle and fully repair the broken trust with the person you were speaking about. You will never be able to explain the full context of the conversation to them or give them the confidence you weren't speaking poorly about them. It will quickly become a game of "he said she said" or a worse, a retaliation cycle.

A good rule of thumb is to never give any thoughts or comments about someone else you wouldn't feel comfortable giving to them directly. And never ever "tattle" on your coworkers or managers. Any feedback you do give should be based on facts and things you can observe-- but keep emotion out of it. Additionally, anything you say should be backed up with a specific example that is not up for debate. And follow it up with a simple recommendation for how the person could do things differently.

Dale Carnegie wrote the book *How to Win Friends and Influence People* many years ago, and it's just as relevant today as the day it came out. One of his initial teachings in that book follows along with the principle: "you get more bees with honey," meaning that you should make it a practice to never criticize, condemn, or complain. It is very easy during performance check-ins and meetings with leadership to complain about what could be, to condemn others for their actions, or to criticize the way a project is being run. Criticizing, condemning, and complaining are not "honey." It's more like vinegar, and it doesn't solve any problems. Avoiding these three important C's will also set a boundary with others and establishes you will always take the high road.

While you are making sure you're not criticizing, condemning, or complaining, think instead of a new strategy you can deploy during these conversations. Focusing on the three S's will ensure you are keeping the conversation productive. These S's are: Solve, Support, and Serve. If you focus on solving problems, being supportive, of all your coworkers and leadership, and serving others to help them solve their greatest problems, your conversations will be as effective as they can possibly be.

Never Reveal Your Masterplan

Often, the career path that your company is envisioning for you is at odds with your Masterplan. Usually, it's something that solves a narrow problem for them but doesn't actually help you build the comprehensive set of skills that will allow you to advance. It is not your manager's responsibility to train or develop you, and definitely not if it's going to make you a valuable asset to another person to another company. Their goal is simply to get the most out of you in your role or an expanded role within their organization. That's why check-ins, reviews, and career planning conversations can be especially treacherous.

You never want to reveal the "Masterplan" to them. Providing them full transparency as to your goals and objectives can hurt you if they don't align with what they are envisioning.

So, keep your "Masterplan" to yourself. And don't overshare.

Maintaining control over your workday is of paramount importance. A great deal of control is enacted just by making sure you are curating the messages you are delivering to others. Curating those messages in a way that keeps subjective opinions to yourself, negative opinions to yourself, or criticisms of others to yourself is imperative. If you are unable to execute a strategy of keeping many of your thoughts close to the vest, then it's highly likely at one time or another you will be categorized as "someone who isn't a team player," "can't get along with others," or "doesn't believe in the mission of the company." Anyone of these three perceptions-- let alone all of these three perceptions-- could slow your career trajectory.

Letting leaders, coworkers, or employees know what you really think puts them in control, and you never want them to be in control. You must be cautious and measured and calculating about what you share, when you share it, and whom you share it with.

TAKE HOME LESSONS:
- Sharing your true feelings can put you in a dangerous situation where a manager, influencer, or other company decision-makers think you are a complainer, difficult to get along with, or don't fit in. These things are all very bad perceptions you want to avoid and can expose you to a layoff or worse.
- Performance reviews and check-ins are events where you want to avoid sharing your true feelings. Your relationship with your manager can result in letting your guard

down and find you giving feedback about your peers, your manager, your boss's boss, or other leaders that are best kept to yourself.
- Avoid sharing your true feelings about tense coworker relationships, it gives the impression you aren't a good collaborator, and may involve you in 'he said, she said' cycles, which are lose-lose in all situations.

ACTION ITEM: In the next meeting you attend, regardless of its effectiveness, end the meeting by thanking the organizer and telling them how valuable the meeting was. Shoot a message to their manager and compliment the organizer. Attract bees with honey...

CHAPTER V
DON'T INVEST IN "LOW ROI" INTERNAL RELATIONSHIPS, FOCUS ON HIGH RETURN EXTERNAL ONES

Looking back on my career, one mistake I've made more than once has minimized my earning potential more than anything else I can think of. This mistake was focusing on building a network of relationships where I was working, instead of making connections outside of my workplace.

By definition of working in a corporate environment, you will develop so many relationships anyway. As long as you're thoughtful about the types of people you're choosing to connect with, there's no harm in getting to know people. My mistake was that I tried to get to know everybody. When the reality was, it was my boss (and my boss's boss) who were the real influencers. None of the other people mattered. They were just the peanut gallery.

I would spend time cultivating deep relationships with my coworkers, both professionally and socially. I would network in the organization both up and down the food chain, having coffees with as many people as it could, going to as many happy hours as I needed to, sacrificing time with my family to go to work dinners. I thought I was doing the right thing. When actually, I was consistently ignoring what I should have been focusing on: opportunities to build relationships outside of my company.

Eventually, when I left that company, I saw the impact of my mistake. I didn't have a good network of contacts to fall back on. Unfortunately, when I really needed those relationships to help me find a new role in a new company or to create a customer base for my consulting business, I didn't have a network that was broad enough or strong enough to tap into. And the most brutal lesson: people from old jobs won't help you find new ones or give you consulting work. Your warts have been exposed, and you've likely been pigeonholed anyway.

It took me two different full-time jobs, being part of five different rounds of layoffs, and consulting independently full-time for two years for it to really hit home how important developing contacts and relationships really are. Each time, I didn't focus enough on myself and instead was focused on the wellbeing of the company and trying to build internal advocates that would help me get ahead.

Early in my career, when things started to turn ugly during my first company turnaround, this was an extreme example of needing contacts and not having them. Day after day of sitting through risk management evaluations where everyone's character was being questioned, and business reviews where it was obvious the deck was stacked against me. The oppressive legal oversight made execution impossible, and success was nonexistent. Months before I left the company, it really hit me. I realized I didn't have an out strategy.

I knew it wasn't going to be simple to look for a new job, and that I would be starting from the ground up. The economy wasn't the greatest at the time, and the job market was extremely competitive. I realized that my search would be from square one, looking for jobs posted on the Internet and trying to get past the company's screening systems that are used to weed out bad candidates. The prospect of this was so overwhelmingly depressing that I just ignored it entirely and decided to double down on making it work at this company no matter how bad the odds were. All this did was to feed into my own frustrations and anxieties about how unsuccessfully everything was going, which made it even worse. Instead of facing this head-on, the problem was compounded even more when I was laid off and had to scramble to build these relationships as fast as I could.

My loss was twofold: Not only didn't I have a good network of contacts when I left the company, but I also didn't open myself up to opportunities at another company where I would have been able to receive more compensation, a better role, or a more appropriate title.

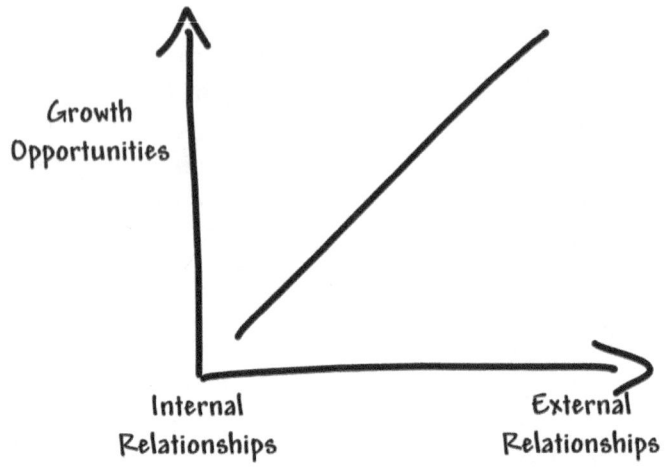

Tell me, if you get a promotion inside your company-- how much is that really worth? Maybe a 2.5% or 3.5% increase in pay? What I'm trying to say is that the incremental value of internal networking is really low. Many companies have capped raises with promotions that keep you continually making less than you should be.

At your current company, you may only be able to get a 7% pay raise. On the other hand, if you were to switch companies, you could make a significant jump up in pay. Maybe 20% or 30% more. If you spend all your time trying to get someone to whisper good things about you in your boss's ear so you can get a promotion, at the end of the day, you're still in the corporate ecosystem. Everyone involved in determining your new salary knows what you're making, and they're going limit your pay raise as much as they can.

The benefit of making connections outside of your company is that when you go to negotiate your next job, you can put yourself in a much better position to negotiate. We even see trends in places like California, where they are protecting employee's salary histories through legislation. A hiring company can't ask you for your salary history, which means you should be able to negotiate a bigger leap in pay.

We've all seen people go from company to company, and often times they come in at a higher level than they've ever achieved before. At the same time, you see someone more qualified in another role, and they have to move heaven and earth just to get to the same position as that person from the outside. Because outside candidates are in greater control of setting their value, external connections hold a higher ROI than internal ones. Internal relationships are with people that are just trying to make you happy enough to stay. There's a big difference between making you happy to stay, and making you happy to make you happy.

You have to start thinking of your relationships in terms of ROI. What's your return on investment for every relationship you develop? The more influence they have on the outside, then the higher the dollar sign. Outside is where it's at. So reallocate all that effort, and don't over-focus on internal stakeholders and such. Anytime you are thinking of developing those internal relationships, spend time developing external (higher yielding) ones instead. When you're at your job, the focus should be on your work and getting it done, freeing up time to build relationships on the outside so you can get your next bump up in salary. And don't focus so much on that promotion your company keeps putting you through the wringer to get.

Mentors, Influencers, and Allies

Over the long course of my career, I figured out something that a lot of other people have known for a very long time, but that a great many of us quieter or more introverted personality types take a lot longer to discover. So much of your life fulfillment, happiness, and success is determined by the relationships you have and how much you put into those relationships.

Helping others and guiding them whenever you can eventually come back and be repaid. Some people call it karma, and some people just say 'what goes around comes around.' But if you help people, people will eventually help you.

Some people are naturals at this type of reciprocity. Rose was one of them.

Rose and I worked together for probably only two or three weeks. I think we were in a grand total of one meeting together during the course of that time. But when she was laid off, she sent me a LinkedIn message to connect. LinkedIn recommends you not connect with people you don't know very well, but I've always thought that's the wrong strategy. Even if you connect with people you don't know, you may discover a way to help them, or you may be able to reach out to them so they can help you. So, I accepted her connection request.

Eight or nine months later, she sent me a message asking if I would be willing to talk to her about preparing for a job interview for a job that was well outside her comfort zone or experience. I responded that I was happy to get on the phone with her, actually expecting that she probably wouldn't follow-up with me, or would be able to work out a mutually agreeable time. Over the course of two or three weeks, we played phone tag, but she was very persistent and didn't give up.

When we finally connected, she had a host of questions that she was looking for specific answers to. She'd prepared thoroughly for our call together and was ready at a moment's notice to begin digging in so she could help herself with the answers I was able to give her. She needed specific answers on how to approach a conversation about the job responsibilities, and how to think about the challenges the business would face and to make sure she was keeping the big picture in mind.

By the end of the call she told me she felt significantly more able to carry on a detailed conversation confidently, credibly, and with an ability to get to the heart of the challenges and opportunities of the position.

So did she get the job? I actually have no idea. Maybe she did, maybe she didn't. I do know that with the information I gave her, she let me know she got past the first round and was able to make a compelling case. The power of the story is to highlight the fact that working hard to develop extra relationships, and being ready to maximize the conversation at a moment's notice is incredibly important and could make the difference between success or failure.

I also know that whether or not it's Rose who does it, helping her is a selfish tactic that will be paid back to me at some point. And wherever she gets rehired, I will have a powerful ally in a company outside of my own.

Start with Your Boss, and Then Your Boss's Boss

I know I'm not the only one who has repeated this mistake. I consistently see people who work very hard at building their internal corporate network but aren't applying any energy to networking outside of their company. Most people approach networking by trying to cultivate relationships with as many people as they can instead of strategically identifying a small number of people inside your company and outside of it that could have a significant positive impact on your career and professional growth.

People worry about negative comments being made behind their back to their boss, but you shouldn't. Not everyone is going to like you or be best friends with you. It's easily handled by not getting defensive and simply saying something along the lines of, "Yeah, not surprising. That person is always really negative in meetings and doesn't seem to be someone who likes to collaborate with others."

It is far better to have deep relationships with a small number of people than it is to have superficial relationships with a very large number of people. And even if you can have deeper relationships with a large number of people, the reality is most of those people are not in a position to significantly influence your career positively or negatively.

Each person should reallocate time, effort, and energy they're spending on meeting a large number of people to instead developing very deep relationships to just four people inside (and the four people outside) your organization.

Organizing these efforts is very important. You don't want to develop relationships with people that can't influence your career, or be a mentor to you in some way. You should thoughtfully pick 3 to 4 people who are going to be the greatest influencers.

Whether you like it or not, the first person is your boss. I can think back to the jobs where I was most effective, the jobs where I had the most latitude to do what I needed, and the jobs where I was most trusted. Each of those jobs correlated with a deep relationship with my manager.

Connecting with your manager on a personal level is critically important and will help you understand and predict their personality as well as their motivating factors and what they are trying to accomplish professionally for themselves. This is important knowledge that can be used in a positive way to drive alignment between you both and make sure you are providing value.

The second person on your list should be your boss's boss. Even if your direct manager is an advocate for you, they still need their manager to be supportive of the company's investment in you and to support promotions and raises.

Having a personal connection with your boss's boss also may open you up to unexpected growth opportunities that will allow you to build new skills. The last one or two people who you should develop relationships with are influencers of your manager. You should be someone who has the ear of your manager and is trusted by your manager. These should be peers of your boss, so they carry enough credibility to make a difference.

Find People Who Can Hire You

Networking and relationship building outside of your company have different considerations. At the companies you would be interested in working for, identify decision-makers or people in hiring positions who may have roles you could see yourself in. Additionally, try to find some individuals who are at a similar place in their career or a similar level in their career. The goal of networking with these people is to develop relationships with people who may make you aware of jobs and are also more accessible than the hiring managers.

With your external network, you will have to be more diligent in maintaining the relationships. It won't be as easy to meet with them consistently, but if your interactions are not consistent, the relationship will not be able to move to the next level. If you're not able to move the relationship to a personal one, and one that is consistent, when you ask for information about opportunities it will appear inauthentic and the likelihood of them helping you is very low.

When building your relationships externally, you have to be thoughtful of how many people you're extending to. It is different than being inside and trying to uncover the greatest opportunities within a company, you have to talk with more people. Building a deeper connection with each person will still critical, and it becomes harder as you expand your network. It's best to create a system where you can track who you are talking to and make sure you are following up with them and thinking proactively about opportunities to connect.

Make Yourself Useful to Others

In all these interactions, you can ground yourself by focusing on one mantra: be valuable. As you're developing your relationships, work to uncover what challenges these people may face and what needs they have. Work actively to help solve their problems directly, or connect them to a solution.

Help them without an expectation that you will get anything in return. If this is done from a place of authenticity, with no expectations, it is guaranteed that the people you help will return the favor. The forces of reciprocity exist within each of us, and when someone does something helpful for us, we automatically feel the need to pay it back. That payback will naturally happen over time.

While it does take significantly more diligence than it would appear to be on the surface, planning out your outreach, tracking it, and managing your time effectively will result in great opportunities. Making sure you don't have all of your eggs in one basket, and you broaden your network both inside and outside of your company gives you the greatest opportunities for the advancement of your career.

TAKE HOME LESSONS:
- The worst mistake is to only develop relationships inside the company you currently work for. It severely limits your professional opportunities.
- Inside your current company, you only need 3-4 close relationships to affect your career positively. Any additional effort you are

giving should be reallocated to building your outside relationships.
- When you target outside relationships, start with 3-4 with the intention of rapidly developing others. You will have to leverage your organizational skills to keep track of conversations, follow-ups, and the needs you uncover as you talk to them. Ask your new relationships for who else you should talk to, and talk to them often.
- Rather than focusing on how people can help you, focus on how you can help them. Think through their problems or challenges and connect them to solutions. Payback will naturally happen the more you help people, and as your value increases.

ACTION ITEM: Reach out to your boss's best influencer and ask them to have coffee to get to know them better and learn what their greatest challenges or concerns are.

CHAPTER VI
NEVER BRING SOMEONE ELSE'S IDEA TO REALITY

"This webcast is a nightmare. I can't believe we agreed to do this," my colleague blurted out to me. I could see her hands trembling.

She was talking about an idea I had for a webcast where people could just hop on and watch a customer demonstrating the product live. It was a really cool idea in theory, but in reality, required a huge amount of set up. This was back in the "Golden Age of the Internet"; it was ambitious for the time. Even the idea of a live demo was an 'out there' idea.

"The plan doesn't even make any sense," she lamented. "The technology doesn't work right, and the timelines are too tight."

I felt bad for her, but there wasn't much I could do. I had conceived the idea months earlier, and right after I won an innovation award for it, I immediately got moved off that brand to a new position in the company. So, she was stuck carrying my idea to fruition.

To her credit, she figured out how to do it. She recruited people, organized the entire project, and pulled it off. But she hated it, and it was a massive pain in the ass. While she was able to get the project on track, it took a Herculean effort and distracted her from other priorities that were on her plate. In the end, the final product met expectations of her leadership team, but it didn't give her the boost to her career that she was hoping for.

And after all her hard work, all she really got was a pat on the back and a 'job well done.' She didn't get the recognition or rewards that she should have. Much of the credit went to me, the innovator.

When you're put in the situation where you are delivering a product or concept for others, you are at risk for some critical things. You risk underachieving versus their vision or goal, you risk impossible or missed timelines, you risk bad blood between you and the creator of the idea, and you risk a significant amount of stress. For these reasons, I believe you should avoid bringing another person's idea to reality as much as possible.

But some of the most common things people say to me is: Shouldn't I deliver what my stakeholders want and make them happy? Isn't that a sure way to get promoted and get recognized?

You're never going to make them happy in this type of situation. If you want success you have to make sure you're not just guessing in any circumstance, and that things are being driven by you and not another person. But that's exactly the opposite of what is happening if you're bringing another person's idea to reality. You will always be guessing, and you still won't make your stakeholders happy no matter what you do. Trying to read someone's mind is a recipe for two things: disaster and underachievement. It's a no-win situation because no matter how hard you work, the person who created the idea will always think they could've done it better, faster, or easier.

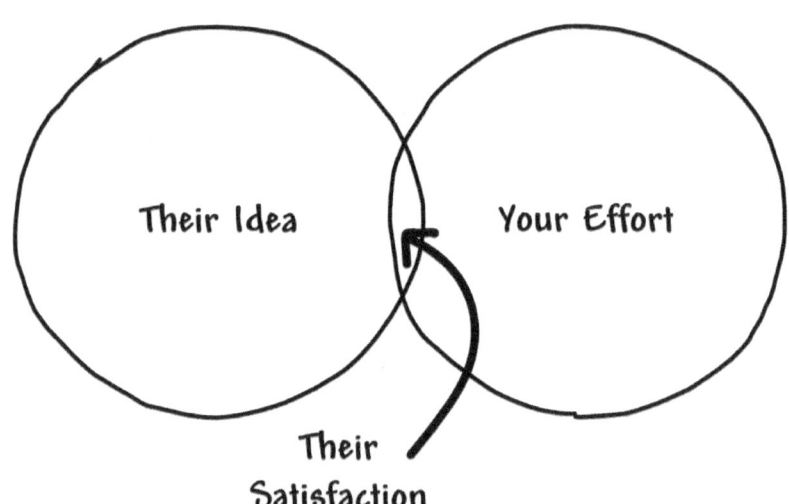

They'll Always Think They Could Have Done It Better

I find this a lot with other stakeholders: particularly in matrix organizations where the requestor isn't the one doing the work They'll see what a competitor is doing and want you to do the same thing. Usually, this isn't a great idea, it doesn't solve an actual business problem, and as a result, there is no real reason for it-- but they want it anyway.

For instance, they'll come to you and say, "Our competitor is holding customer dinners, we need to do that too!" Or, "The competition is giving away free samples!"

Now all the employees are trying to run customer dinners and give away product just to match what the other guy is doing. You know your stakeholders aren't going to like it. It's a rip off of someone else, and it won't be exactly the same as the competitors. And when you turn in your first proposal they'll start by saying it's not good enough, and they'll continue to critique you, even though they couldn't effectively develop the program or materials on their own, and usually are unable to execute effectively in the field to maximize the new tool. Suddenly it hits home-- you're doing something that has no business rationale and doesn't solve any real problem other than giving someone something they think they want. You've become a doer, not a thinker. Now you're just reactive.

For some reason, when I tell people they should avoid taking on projects such as these, I get a lot of pushback. This is because most people are not managing their career or their job responsibilities and want an easy way out. They're letting their career path be dictated by others. It's easy to try to be a people pleaser and think that it will pay off. Maybe you'll get a promotion: but you won't get two. And you'll wake up one day and realize you are at the beck and call of someone else. It's the opposite of our Selfish Career goals. Unfortunately, it's difficult getting away from this cycle, and people are confronted with this type of situation routinely. This entire book is designed to give you the tools you need to avoid doing someone else's dirty work; however, even the greatest execution of a "Selfish Career" cannot prevent this from happening occasionally.

Prepare for the Inevitable (At some point we all have to do it)

Invariably, you will be faced with a situation where you cannot avoid bringing another person's idea of reality. When this happens, you have to force yourself to employ a 'checkbox mentality' to get to the project successfully completed. The first step in doing this is to understand the specific requirements. Understanding the specific requirements will at least give you the knowledge of why you were doing what you were doing.

The first step in this process is asking "why?"

There is a great book written by Simon Sinek called *Start with Why*. He states that when you begin by asking the question of why, rather than how or what, it will give you the greatest opportunity for success because it will ground everyone in the mission and the ultimate goal. I would suggest reading his book to understand the background and why this is. If you don't have time for full reading, search for his videos of the same name around the web which explain it adequately.

But here's a synopsis. Let's say you get saddled with delivering an idea that someone else came up with. Instead of asking them how they want it to look, or how to carry out the plan, diagnose the problem that they trying to solve, so you can credibly go back to them with a version of what they want. Instead of focusing on the solution, focus on the problem we're trying to solve. It gives you a little bit more flexibility, in that you won't have to try and guess exactly what's in their mind.

By asking 'why' you're also resetting their expectations. You're not saying, "No. I won't explore your idea." You're letting them know that you're going to do your best to solve the business problem, in a way that makes sense to you. Remember, they're not going to be happy anyway, so the real goal here is to get it off your plate as quickly as you can, so you can move onto the next version of the idea, that you *can* control.

Everybody is an Expert

The inherent problem with bringing another person's idea to life is the everybody is an expert. Most people look at their jobs and think it is significantly more difficult or complex than someone else's job. It doesn't matter what it is, but most people are so self-focused they don't understand what goes into each individual's expertise across the functional areas within an organization. Because of that, they generally think that they can do your job better than you can.

This is a fundamental reason why bringing the idea of another person to reality is complex and difficult and why it's so easy to underperform their expectations. As you navigate this process, there are some key tips and tricks that will help make sure you don't underperform. I mentioned earlier you should start with why and understand very clearly what this new idea is trying to accomplish, but there are others that will help you as well. They are questions you can ask that will help you become more in control of the project rather than just executing an idea someone else thought of.

The first tactic is to have a conversation around what determines success or failure. What would the project look like if it was successful, and what would it look like if it failed? Additionally, ask how the project should be evaluated. Engaging in debate around how something will be assessed is a key to making sure you have analytics that will help establish objectively that the program was a success or failure. This will also help you check the box to make sure that the metrics and evaluation criteria have been achieved without pushing them further than is needed and taking time away from your other priorities.

Asking and evaluating how much your 'bright idea' colleague knows about the subject or tactic they're asking you to do is also very important, as this will ensure that they are aware that they don't know much about the subject and couldn't do it on their own if they wanted to. You will have to get into details around the project plan to make sure that they fully see the difference between a rookie and an expert.

Lastly, there are bound to be requests or requirements that are nearly impossible to achieve. You'll have to employ the tactic of using 'no, but.' Using the phrase 'No, but' allows you to establish a boundary on what can be achieved and then allows you to suggest a different, more realistic course of action that the person can agree to. This will keep your project from becoming too difficult to execute and make sure that the plan is achievable.

Get as Many Specifics as Possible

The next step in this process is to ask for specific requirements. People who create ideas will have specifics in mind and they should be able to articulate those that may be how the project comes to life, the look and feel of materials, or may involve the employment of a specific strategy or tactic that they believe will make the project more successful. If they can't articulate any requirements, you can use this as a stopping point to push back until they do. Sometimes the projects go away at this point.

You will have to ask a variety of questions to understand specifically what these requirements might be since they will be critically important to make sure they are incorporated. If you do not incorporate these specific requirements, often the idea creator will be very negative about how the project was ultimately completed. It is better to implement the specific requirements rather than trying to convince the person who created the idea that their methods aren't valid or don't work.

Remember to "Play the Game"

Remember the chapter on playing the game; this is a perfect example of needing to employ that strategy.

So, how do we "Play the Game" here?

You're not being argumentative about the project. You've tried to get rid of it by trying to understand the business purpose and investigating 'why.' You have an open dialogue going with the creator of the idea, and you realize they'll never give up on it. Now is the time to reorient on the issue and turn in a minimally viable product, assuming you've managed their expectations. Tell them the idea is good, that their feedback is valuable, and you appreciate it. In other words, don't make waves. Go in there and nod when they give you feedback. You don't have to be jumping up and down excited, but don't continue to grumble or tell them that it's stupid. Adopt a customer service mindset.

Get Confirmation

While you want to make sure you're spending enough time and effort on making sure that the project is successful the focus needs to be on accomplishing the essentials and the minimums to make sure you can bring it to life and close the book on what is likely a lower value project. A key nuance to executing these projects is to not waste time and effort on making this program spectacular when you could make your own idea spectacular. During the execution you want to maintain a high level of check-in's, you want to get them committed to the plan and program, to minimize unnecessary changes along the way, and you want to focus on achieving those checkboxes. Upon execution and finalizing the project, you want to increase your communication with the idea generator, so you're reminding them the service you've provided and confirming that they believe that the project was executed effectively.

Some of the most personally satisfying experiences I've had is recommending against a course of action on a project, being overruled, bringing it to market under precise direction by a stakeholder and watching it fail. After this, it's much easier to push back and kill the next dumb idea. It's proof that sometimes you just have to play the game, and let the situation play out. But assuming you played the game in a savvy fashion, you are now free to take it to the next level if it has potential.

Take it to the Next Level, Improve on the Idea

If the fundamental idea could be good, evaluate its potential, whether or not you want to take it to the next level. Taking the project to the next level would be worthwhile if you were able to take the foundation of what you've built by checking the boxes and amplify it significantly. You would only want to do this if you could separate the ownership of the original idea from the person who created it in the first place. You would have to be able to make it so much better than the original idea that you can gain control of the idea itself and could execute it on your own terms and with your own vision and not be restricted by the person who created it.

While I would recommend that the better thing to do is to create your own idea, I recognize that sometimes you have momentum on the ideas of others, and you can use it as a springboard to something that will allow you to learn a new skill and continue your personal development process, and be rewarded at the same time.

"That's stupid" (Sell Your Own Idea Instead)

Sometimes-- albeit very rarely-- you can inject your own idea before you get saddled with someone else's.

Let's go back to the business problem. If you've established the 'why' and you see that there's a better solution at hand to solve this problem logically, this would be the time to sell them your own idea instead.

Ideally, the better way to go is to proactively create ideas that no one's thought of. To do this, you have to consistently engage stakeholders who are routinely in the position to create ideas for you. You need to dialog with them about the challenges that they face and what they're trying to achieve. If you are doing this, you will be able to create solutions and ideas that they didn't think of. If you are smart enough to be reading this book, and you work to understand the problems deeply, your ideas are sure to be better than theirs.

I found most people not to be horribly creative and will generally recycle the same things over and over again, or will want to replicate something they've seen someone else do. So brainstorm on solutions, gain alignment with the stakeholders and leadership, and use a number of people to all support a solution you have come up with. Try to drive to a couple solutions that could solve the problem and put people in a forced choice situation with a have to choose one or the other commit to it and abandon all other random ideas.

So, how do we sell them a new idea? By creatively engineering the new solution to be faster to market, you may have a shot at swaying them off their original idea entirely.

In other words, you have to establish that not only can it be solved differently, but you can solve their real problem faster with your new idea. You're also trying to suggest that if you bring your solution to reality sooner and it doesn't work, then you'll have time to explore other ideas they had.

The catch is that you just need the confidence that your idea is the better idea.

Of course, all this takes effort, you have to be smarter and use your brain and come up with better solutions. But the whole premise of this book is for people who are trying to maximize those smarts, set themselves up for success, and give themselves the most freedom in their job by outthinking others. So, if you really don't want to get stuck with the shitty end of the deal, trying to execute on a kooky idea, and when it's all done, you got nothing more than a pat on the back-- get that brain working!

I'll Pass...

In the rare event that you do get to turn down a project where you'd be carrying out someone else's idea, you'll need to do this tactfully. If you're able to turn it down, the easiest trick is to get your boss involved, and have your boss tag team the person with you and try to get it off your plate. You can assist in this process by listing out other more important things that are of higher priority. In other words, "If you want us to do this thing, then these other two projects are going to have to be parked." Another avenue is to walk them through your budget or suggest other important items be cut from it.

Many people are uncomfortable with that. They want *everything* like it's an all-you-can-eat buffet.

Forcing them into tradeoff choices is critical, but some people will refuse and will tell you to 'do it all.' You'll have to continue ratcheting down expectations, letting them know that you can do all the projects all at once, but that in all likelihood they'll end up with three crappy projects instead of one that's really good. If they still insist you go ahead, then consider turning in three substandard projects to show them how their decisions affect work quality. Whoever you're working with will likely say-- "oh, they said they can't do three projects at the same time, I see now."

Don't worry about getting fired for turning in crappy work. Especially if you've managed their expectations. It's very likely that you will learn the amount of effort and work quality you put into your work is much higher than needed. If they accept it without batting an eyelash, you'll realize their expectations are much lower than you thought. That's a good thing! The next time you work with them, you can turn in lower quality work because that's all they know. And we're back to the selfishness of using your time judiciously.

TAKE HOME LESSONS:
- Bringing another person's idea to reality typically results in underperforming against expectations because you aren't a mind reader.
- When you have to bring another person's idea to reality, apply a checkbox approach where you quickly fulfill their project needs without additional effort
- Move as rapidly as possible to a phase two where you can amplify the original idea but put your creative spin on it. Don't do this until the first phase is completed, and the lame idea has been launched or released.

ACTION ITEM: Think of a business partner that routinely requests idiotic ideas. Come up with a proactive solution and present it to them to get them focused on an idea you can control when you bring it to reality.

CHAPTER VII
DON'T GET CAUGHT WITHOUT A LONG-TERM PLAN

Passive employees get passed up.

When you think of most competitive sports— basketball, football, soccer— the aggressor always wins. That's what you need to understand. You have to be the aggressor. If you are always on the defensive, in sports, your life, and definitely in your career, then you fail. You must be executing against a long-term plan, at all times, and pushing the envelope.

This goes back to what we discussed in the previous chapter: passive and reactive vs. proactive. For success to happen, you can't be a passenger. Connect directly to the results. So many people are caught in the corporate trap of being a "Drone," afraid they're going to make someone mad at them, or rock the boat. They won't risk it. You can't just go along, constantly hoping things will work out or wanting to please people. The only way you should be pleasing people is by turning in kick-ass work. Not because you have a subservient, people pleaser attitude. A CEO once told me, "I don't want to work with the person who admires my job. I want the person who *wants* my job."

Develop a long-term plan where you evaluate the business situation, build out what you want to accomplish, and execute on it. Getting the ball rolling on this is very important. So, when someone comes to you with a shiny ball; a worthless distraction, you can prevent them from adding "junk" work onto your plate. Otherwise, you're just passively drifting by, letting other people dictate your day, and constantly bringing other people's ideas to reality. Remember, this book isn't just about getting new skills and promotions, it's also about you having control of your day, making sure you are driving your destiny, and not someone else.

I know it's hard to swallow, but you're not going to get this advice anywhere else, because these are the things that people aren't supposed to say. *People aren't supposed to be selfish.*

The key to this is just simply taking a step back and carving out the time to build out a proactive plan. A lot of people don't do that. They come up with excuses instead. They say they are too busy. But the point I'm trying to make is that when you're thinking more about the future than everybody else is, you'll be naturally one step ahead of them. You'll be the aggressor who wins the game.

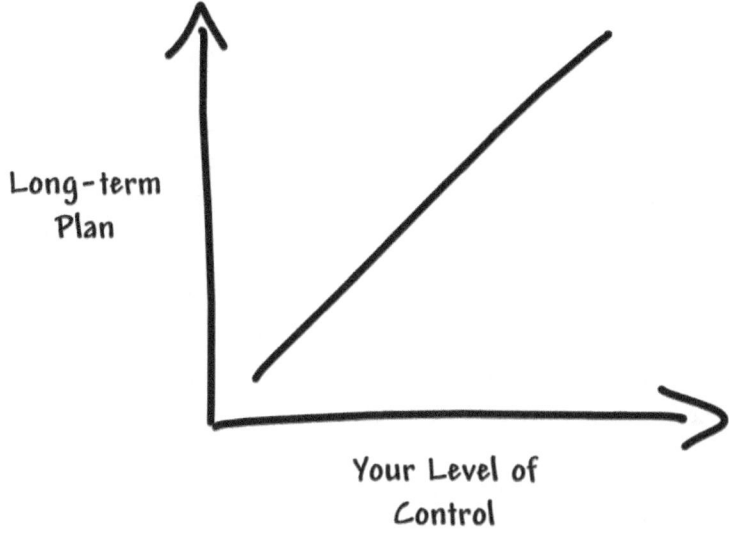

Outthink Leaders and Stakeholders with a Longer Plan than they Expect

"So happy to have these new sales aids...they are great," the sales VP said. "We've begun to use them, and they are really working out well. You actually gave us more than we needed. Now, what we need next is a video and some new white papers, and I think some journal ads would really help too!"

I never worked harder for less results that year. But it was the last time I didn't develop a longer and more detailed plan than what was originally asked for. I spent the next six months creating tactics that were other people's ideas, assets that I didn't agree with and knew wouldn't affect the market and generally didn't get any credit for doing. It was all because I had no way to push back. I had no way to push back because I had no alternatives to propose that were better. I hadn't looked into the real problems they were trying to solve. In other words, I was a short order cook.

Often when I'm coaching or mentoring my team and other colleagues, they will ask me why they shouldn't just work in lockstep with leaders and other requestors. Why do we need to develop a longer-term plan? The main reason is that it violates "Selfish Career Rule #1" to be in control of your own projects and not constantly taking orders from others. I've also learned the hard way that the lockstep approach usually results in lower achievement against both business and personal goals. And it definitely doesn't establish you as a leader.

If you are at the beck and call of the requests of others, you aren't in control of your day or your career. It will force you to be reactive and doesn't really show off your best ideas. To be perceived as someone who is thoughtful, proactive, and is out-thinking others at a higher level, you have to actually be out-thinking others at a higher level. You have to get ahead of the game.

It's Wise to Get Ahead of the Game

There are a number of steps that are required to break the cycle and get ahead of the game.

I've learned over time that people don't understand how to break the cycle. No matter what they do, they are stuck in a situation where other people are giving them one new project after the other and forcing them to be reactive. As I described above it is very easy to wind up in a situation where there's always something being added to your plate rather than taking control of the situation and strategically taking on tasks that will help you develop the skills and experiences you are looking to build.

After a few of these bad experiences where I was being asked to deliver more and more tactics that were not of interest to me and that I knew were not going to help us be successful, I began approaching my job and the execution of tactics in a very different way.

By my third big company, I learned my lesson enough times, and I perfected implementing a long-term plan.

I made sure I took feedback from my stakeholders and outlined their first set of requests. Those requests were for things that they had been sorely lacking and could use my help in setting up a foundation for a better approach. While I was working with an agency and other internal shared service groups to complete the tactics and activities that were needed, that's when I began developing a longer-term and more comprehensive plan.

Any job has a set of challenges or problems that need to be solved. The first step is to assess the situation, understand and document the problems the business is facing, and develop recommendations for action. That's it. Once you've developed a recommendation, flesh out a process plan, and an implementation plan. And then, within that plan, you have different activities. You have to think like a trauma surgeon. You triage the immediate problems to stabilize the patient and then move to solving the real problems.

Because most people are really just reacting all the time, very often waiting for a stakeholder to tell them what to do, they never get to execute on the types of things that allow them to show off their strengths. Creating a long-term plan establishes you as a planner and a strategic forward thinker. It shows leadership acumen and leadership potential.

I'm continually surprised that even at higher leadership levels, people are playing "whack-a-mole." Waiting for problems to arise and then trying to tackle them, while waiting for the next one to pop up. When you're in that mode, you can never rest. Because you're constantly "whacking down" problems that are arising, you're never in control of your day, your week or your month. This is why a lot of people end up working on their vacations. Because they're not executing against the plan, they're just playing "whack-a-mole."

Outthinking leaders isn't that hard. Most are too wrapped up their own concerns, believing in their own headlines and B.S. If you can commit to getting off the hamster wheel for a minute and take a proactive mindset towards your own personal end goal of freedom from the whims of others, then you can get there. But if you're worried about making every VP happy and hoping they 'like' you, then your career will be a perpetual uphill climb.

When you develop a plan and execute against it, problems pop up a lot less. There are less "moles" to whack. And problems tend to be less immediate, it's easy to tell which are important and which are just distractions.

Use the Plan to Push Back on Bad Ideas

Once you begin executing on your plan, there are bound to be times where others will throw a monkey wrench into it. Maybe they want to use a tactic that they've seen competitors do or an idea that someone else has suggested. When this happens, force them to make tough choices and identify which items and activities that are in your plan that should be eliminated and make them answer why.

This forces them to feel the pain of trade-offs. If they want something added, then something must be taken away. If your plan is good enough and your tactics are valuable, then they're going to be faced with some very tough decisions.

There will be a tendency to try and deliver the replaced items anyway. If you continue to deliver both their new ideas and the tactics you had to deprioritize you're setting up a situation for yourself where you will be continuously taken advantage of. You must make them feel the pain of their choices. This is how people lose control of their days, weeks, or months so easily. Trying to accomplish too many things reduces quality and results in a lot of effective tactics.

The first time I successfully implemented a long-term plan, I made sure I mapped out a strategy that was 2 to 3 years out. While the foundational tactics were entering the market, we began building more advanced tactics for release shortly on the heels of the foundational ones. As others tried to suggest different tactics that they thought we needed, I was able to walk them back to the plan and show them that what we had developed was significantly more advanced and would solve their problems better. Not only did it keep us from doing things that weren't effective and weren't going to help us build new skills, it also had a more positive effect on the business because we had evaluated the overall market situation. The result was that we were able to stay ahead of the game, while everybody else was on the defensive.

Don't Copy a Failed Experiment (do your research)

One of the worst things you can do is develop a plan without knowing what has been unsuccessful in the past and propose something that has failed before. This creates a credibility problem, and you will lose any faith your internal and external customer has in your ideas. Avoid proposing plans that haven't worked before, even if you believe you could fix them and make it work. Even if something wasn't executed effectively, you'll be fighting an uphill battle to prove that it could work if it were executed differently.

The first thing you need to be able to accomplish this goal is to understand the foundation or the background of the overall situation. You have to dig in and understand the business objectives, and what needs to be accomplished at a very deep level. You can't have superficial knowledge or an incomplete understanding. You have to research it, collect insights about the customer whether they are internal or external. You need to conduct research in the form of formal market research and talk with your customer directly and complete a fact-finding mission to gain as much knowledge as you can. You also have to process research that has been done before, so you know what has worked and what hasn't.

Most people aren't able to differentiate between poor and excellent execution, therefore even if your plan is an improvement on someone else's failed strategy, they will still be very skeptical. Avoiding a failed tactic altogether or not doing it until all other options have been exhausted, is usually the best plan.

How to Create a Phase I, II, and III

Phase I, the foundation plan. First, create new look materials of things that have worked in the past. You can create different versions or new creative expressions of what is essentially the same thing used before and provide advancement to make it better. Build any foundational plan with some basics that everyone agrees on, and will set the groundwork for your overall plan. These are usually tactics that are comparatively easy to accomplish, but everyone will be confident in.

By doing these foundational things first, you'll be able to build your Phase One plan, and it'll be easier to get buy-in from your stakeholders. Once you get buy-in, you can begin to bring them to life. Make sure you're allocating enough time to begin your Phase II planning. Don't spend so much time on creating the tactics that won't be setting yourself up for success over the long term. This is the highest risk point, most people get lost in the day to day and don't focus on the planning.

As you are building the foundational tactics, begin to develop your Phase II plan. Think a step or two ahead of everyone else. You'll have to determine how to build off your foundation of original tactics to keep making Phase II and III bigger and better. You need to make sure that the new tactics for these phases aren't just duplications of the original Phase I tactics but rather new ideas. You need to place new tactics in broad categories you can "ladder up" to the overall business objective, and figure out how it solves a market problem.

Put general timelines together for the different phases and map out a plan that is 1 to 2 years out. Don't be overly specific with the tactics or you can box yourself in. You want to be able to make adjustments based on the new things you are learning as the Phase I activities get in the market.

As you develop your plan, and you begin to carry on discussions with leaders and stakeholders, you will sometimes encounter someone who says, "Don't worry about that." They'll tell you to focus on executing what is on your plate today.

This is a trap!

This is exactly how you stay in the cycle of always being reactive to the demands and needs of other people. If you want to reclaim control of your day, build skills and experiences that are valuable to you, you have to ignore these kinds of statements and continue to polish your plan.

Explain you will be executing all those current tactics, but it's good to spend time creating an ongoing plan, so you are able to move faster and react to the market. If they continue to push back and won't buy into this approach, develop a plan in secret. Your organizational skills, foresight, and ability to fashion an approach that is valuable for you will be rewarded over time. And who knows, they may not even be around in a year or two if they aren't thinking ahead. Alternatively, you might be on to bigger and better things too.

Revealing the Plan

At some point, you'll want to reveal your plan in full.

The best way to reveal a long-term plan is to do it individually. Let's say there are four main stakeholders, you would share the plan to them one at a time. That way, you can collect individual feedback on the plan in a low-risk setting. This lets people poke holes in the plan in a way that helps you make it better, rather than them ganging up on you. As I'm sure you know, a lot of grandstanding occurs in meetings. If you present your ideas and people are around higher-ups, people may want to show off, and they'll do this by tearing down your plan. So, go to them individually and have those conversations, and build in their legitimate concerns one by one.

Do this with all the necessary people you feel you need to do this with. In general, nobody responds negatively to having plans if you are building them their near-term tools too. A thoughtful strategy or a thoughtful way of approaching something with an executable plan is great. Most people just don't do it!

Make sure your plan contains the market research and insights so you can demonstrate a full understanding of the business situation and the tactical approach you plan to use. Walk them through your ideas, so they are forced to react and respond to what you have proposed rather than them giving you different ideas that don't match your agenda of skill development. This insulates you from them giving ideas that don't match the needs of the business or your personal needs and helps them avoid unrealistic ideas. It also puts them in a situation where they have to give concrete reasons why they shouldn't execute what you are proposing. That is much harder than suggesting random ideas that don't make sense. This also allows you to add in some of their ideas to make them feel like they are an active participant in the planning process.

TAKE HOME LESSONS:
- If you work at the pace of others and are always reacting to their plan, you won't get to show off your best ideas. It forces you to react, rather than building the great skills you want.
- Instead, build a proactive plan with a longer runway than expected by others.
- To do this successfully, you have to dig deeply into the problems that need to be solved and come up with a long term plan that is inventive.
- You have to think a step or two ahead of your peers to propose things they must react to, which prevents you from doing the work of others.

- Put the stakeholders on the defensive with the proactive plan and force them into tradeoff choices, forcing them to prioritize and make tradeoffs.

ACTION ITEM:
Block a day on your calendar to work from home and develop a 1-year plan for a very insignificant program or tactical campaign. Force yourself to be creative. Demonstrate to yourself that you can create a longer-term plan. Use that experience to be more confident in tackling a larger initiative that is core to your job and business.

CHAPTER VII
WHEN IN DOUBT, TELL PEOPLE WHAT TO DO

When I began my marketing career, I was the junior most marketer in age and title. There were members of the team with Bachelors and Master's degrees from Harvard, Princeton, University of Chicago, and Northwestern. Not to mention, in marketing experience, I was far behind everyone else. I was even very junior compared to the colleagues I worked with on shared services teams.

Despite being outranked by my colleagues, digging into projects, it became readily apparent that age, experience, title or where your degree was from, had very little to do with your ability to make good decisions or lead. In fact, what I found was that most people wanted, even needed, to be told what to do. If I wanted to succeed, I knew I had to have the courage of my convictions and the willingness to direct people to the right answers and actions.

No one ever got anywhere being a follower. That's the harsh reality. If you don't want to be the one dictating to others, it means you're going to be the one who is dictated to. There's a strong misconception that success will arise from finding out what people want and delivering that exact thing to them. As a result, people too easily take the direction of others and don't shape the projects they're working on themselves. This feeds into the natural inclination to be followers. In fact, if you look at the different Personality types based on the Meyers-Briggs assessments, you will see that the bulk of the population prefers, and takes comfort in, rules, laws, and authority by others.

Unfortunately, if you continue following instead of leading your entire career, you'll likely end up as a professional short order cook who spends his days doing the bidding of others. The first time this clicked for me was early in my career. It was my first job, actually.

My first job after finishing undergrad was as a production chemist. I spent the entire day analyzing samples of water and soil to make sure that they didn't have any harmful chemicals in them. This was a far cry from the job I had imagined when I graduated with a degree in chemistry. I thought I would be inventing groundbreaking new chemicals, not analyzing dirt. Despite that fact, I must have been better at my job than I realized, because not too long after I started, they asked me to oversee a much older colleague. He wasn't very production minded and was always behind, whereas I was organized and always ahead. So they wanted me to do some coaching.

When I first started working with him, I could tell he was resistant. You could see it in his body language. Arms crossed, leaning back on one leg, trying to put as much space between him and me without actually running out the door. At one point, he even said, "I don't know if I can take advice or direction from someone so much younger than me." At least he was honest.

I could've thrown in the towel. I could've given up. But I thought back to all of those times in school, working on group projects with people who always put in the minimum effort, didn't have a unique point of view, and didn't want to take the lead. The last person I wanted to become was someone who spent their life following others. I thought to myself, *what's the difference between the classroom and the office?*

So, instead of folding, I chose to just tell him what to do. And as I migrated from giving advice, to giving more definitive and specific direction, he went from being skeptical and standoffish to just doing the work the way I told him to. I wasn't mean to him; I wasn't ordering him around. But I was clear and concise, committed, and confident.

Over and over, this has proven out during my career. The only difference between the office and the classroom is that in the classroom you are the same age and rank as everyone else, and in the office, there's a perceived difference in experience or competency because of the title. But at its heart, almost all of those people are still the same 'kids in the class' who want to avoid being picked as the leader of the class project.

The Dick Cheney Effect

Many people struggle with the concept of leadership. There is a continual debate about whether leaders are born or made. I figured out how to be the one dictating direction versus having it dictated to me, but I don't particularly think I was predestined for that role. I don't buy into the adage 'we all can be leaders' most companies push either. While I don't think leadership is a quality you possess only when you have the authority or the title to lead, I also don't think it's a skill you have to be born with. Instead, I think of it more tactically. I believe leadership has much more to do with the clarity and confidence in your direction and the presentation of your point of view. Confidence confers leadership.

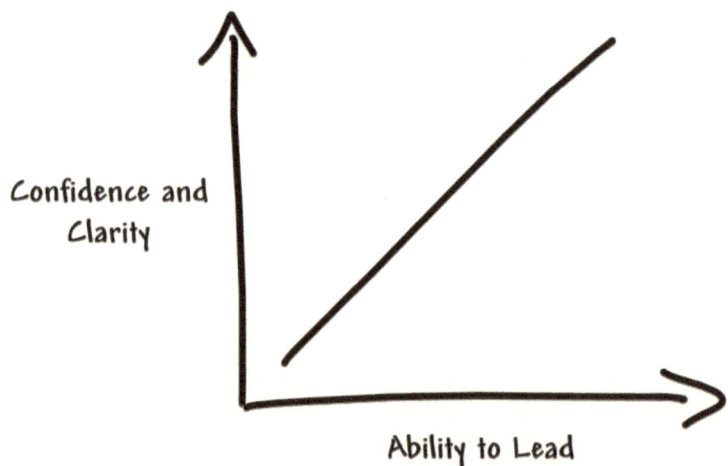

I call this the "Dick Cheney Effect."

Regardless of your political leanings, Dick Cheney is considered the most powerful Vice President in American history for a reason. He had limited real authority to tell people what to do, but he just confidently went in and did it anyway. There is little argument that Cheney summarily redefined what a Vice President could or couldn't do. He surrounded himself with loyal people who enabled him to make those decisions and carry out his plans. This is the type of leadership qualities I'm talking about in this chapter. It's all about confidence. Leadership is in the way you carry yourself: you may not be the president, but you don't have to be a lightweight either.

Taking charge and leading with confidence will naturally establish your authority within your peer group. Others will look up to you and will comment to your leadership about the great job you're doing. You will see that a surprising number of people will still follow you even if they don't agree with what you're doing because the vast majority aren't interested in leading at all. To most people, it's too much hard work to lead and requires a new set of skills that they have to build. This is a big reason why in the absence of leaders, people will follow those that express confidence and clarity.

Usually, when a high degree of confidence is displayed, others will automatically defer regardless of the idea. They may throw up initial concerns but will back down if you double down. But to double down effectively, and gain consensus for your plan, the presentation of your ideas is imperative. If you work to clearly communicate the background, facts, and how you came to a conclusion, you will get significantly more people on board. Full accounting is needed. To give people a full accounting, you must establish clear points of view about the problem you're trying to solve, the options considered, and the course of action you're recommending. This combination results in leaders who rise to the top and maintain control of their personal situations.

Age Actually is Just a Number

The first mental block people have to get over is that age and experience don't mean much at all. Unless age and experience are tied to skill sets you have learned like we discussed in other chapters, age is essentially meaningless. That's because most people don't focus on the development of skills the way we've outlined in this book. Instead, people aimlessly wander through their careers, allowing companies and managers to define for them what they're doing. Because of this, clear direction and leadership is always something that will be expected of you and something you can deliver.

Most of the time, you are going to be working within your peer group, and those peers will often be one level down or one level up from you. That means the people you are working with generally have the same level of authority, so it will be easier for you to find opportunities to lead them. Because you have been strategic in identifying your own personal goals and how you can fit them into what the company needs, and are focused on maintaining as much control of your day as possible, you will have a high incentive to step forward and lead others. Remember: leading others isn't just about the ability to benefit your career, it's also about helping you maintain control of your life and your precious time.

When you confidently tell others what to do, almost everyone you encounter will defer to you. Probably because it's the path of least resistance and most people don't like conflict. Over the course of my career, I have found only a small number of people who have challenged my leadership. Almost universally, the people who bristled at my directions or that I was taking control, were very tenured staff members that happened to be very 'experienced,' or have worked for the company for a very long time.

These people are just "Old Drones." They've been in a holding pattern for most of their career.

For these people, 'experience' really means 'years.' It doesn't convey the same type of experiences that this book covers, which translate into useable and valuable skills. These people are intimidated by younger people who have new ideas but fewer years under their belt. That is because Old Drones have nothing else to lean on other than their years. These are often subject matter experts who know a lot about one small subject but don't see the big picture.

Obviously, these people have not progressed through the organization very effectively and are working low to midlevel jobs even though they think they have something important to add. They are defensive of younger people or anyone who steps up and tries to lead others without authority. They will often exhibit a variety of unproductive and sometimes unprofessional behaviors.

Because they've been Drones for so long they've "seen it all," and because they've seen it all, they naysay. All the things they've seen are ineffective, so when the next person who comes in, even if they have a good idea, the Old Drone has seen so many lame ideas, they'll dismiss it immediately. The favorite mottos of the Old Drone are, "I've seen this before" or "Nothing will change," or "It won't go well," and "Leadership didn't say we could do that."

Old Drone Deactivation Protocol

You have to be very cautious about how you handle these individuals. Because of the longevity with the company, some of them may have developed deep relationships with leadership. You have to investigate and determine whether this is true or not. Usually, you'll find that while the person may have a good relationship, they don't have a lot of credibility because their career is stalled. Leadership naturally gravitates towards high performers and not the ones who are treading water.

If you've determined that the naysayer doesn't have credibility or doesn't have relationship, the easiest strategy is to ignore them. They will usually get anxiety over being left behind and will fall into line.

The more effective strategy, albeit one that takes more energy, is to create a relationship with this person in an effort to have them on your side. They are going to be skeptical of you, and you will not acquiesce to turn over leadership to them, so you need to recognize that developing the relationship may include a variety of roadblocks and speed bumps. Play to their ego, telling them that you need their thoughts and advice and want to learn from them. The Old Drone treading water falls for it every time.

The 80/20 Rule (Why You Should Aim to be in the 20%)

As you lead without authority within an organization or group, you will find you will be increasingly perceived as a leader by others. Because of this fact, it will open up advancement opportunities for you. The caution you must exercise is making sure you don't place the pursuit of titles and advancement over the cultivation of new skills and experiences.

Many people give the advice, "Don't worry about titles...they don't mean anything" as if to imply you should be happy with the level you are at. Unfortunately, titles mean authority, believability, and most importantly, money and control. Don't let others convince you that a title is not important. Titles are important. There's not much reason to work at a lower level and for lower money than you have to for the entirety of your career.

While you are on your journey for skill development and experience collection, don't concern yourself with the titles of your immediate working group peers, though. There will be people one level above and sometimes two that will imply that you should defer to them. Instead, lead them. Leading others without authority helps you build leadership and motivational skills in an organic way, so you don't have to use authority, pressure, or threats to get people to work hard for you. Additionally, it will help you shape your style, practice, and hone it in a lower risk situation. You will be able to experiment and fail with minimal repercussions. Take these leadership opportunities and use them to develop the hard and soft leadership skills and be the person that gets to the heart of the problem, comes up with solutions, and helps implement action plans.

The reality is that it's always better to be leading others than being an order taker executing someone else's plan and has limited control of their day.

I'll leave you a final thought before closing out this short chapter. You must realize that no matter if you are junior or senior in your role, there are 60% of the people you deal with that will be mediocre, 20% are complete buffoons, and the remaining 20% are truly intelligent.

This is the Pareto Principle in action--also known as the 80/20 rule--where 80% of the consequences are from 20% of the causes. I once saw an interview with President Obama where he referred to this. He said when he was an Illinois state senator, he was surprised how many colleagues had no clue what they were doing. When he became a US senator, he was even more shocked that the ratio didn't change. He had an anticipation that as he moved into the top rungs of the US government, that the people he would be dealing with would be smarter and better. He was disappointed. Even more surprisingly, as he became President of the United States, and dealt with world leaders, he found the same thing to be true.

The conclusion is that rank and title have very little to do with intelligence or even work ethic. My own experiences have also proven this out. Over time, what I have seen as I have moved up the food chain and dealt with the most senior leaders in a number of companies that these percentages still hold true. It is the simple fact that allows you the possibility of amazing success, if you recognize that 80% of the people, no matter what your role, are unable to see the bigger picture. I trust, that if you found this book, and if you've made the decision to make your career more about you than the company you are working for, you are at least in the top 20% of the professional population regarding intelligence and work ethic. And because of that, I want you to have the confidence that you can achieve whatever you want if you focus on your skills, and you focus on leading others, who frankly just want to be led by someone else.

TAKE HOME LESSONS:
- Most personality types respond to leaders who speak with confidence and conviction. Most people want to be led, and all you have to do is provide the leadership for them to follow.
- Leading is better than following. No one ever maximized their opportunities or talents by being a great follower. It also ensures you are in greater control of your day and destiny and not executing the ideas of others...another key commandment we covered in the book.
- People inside your working peer group will usually look to others to lead. Ignore titles and step up to the plate.
- Watch out for Old Drones who are 'experienced' in years but not rich in skills. They will resist your leadership. The best tactic is to develop a relationship with them to reduce their resistance or simply ignore them.
- Leading without authority while you are junior allows you to take risks and experiment with your leadership style and allows you to form and hone it in a nearly risk-free way.

ACTION ITEM: At your next working group meeting make a bold proclamation of how you could better accomplish your goals and how to better organize to be more effective. Watch the room for reactions to your conviction and confidence.

CHAPTER IX
ABANDON SHIP WHEN THE COMPANY IS SINKING

"We really need you more than ever. We're going to turn this around, and you're going to be a huge part of that. We need people like you who can think differently and push us through past this little bump in the road. You'll probably get a promotion or even two because of it!"

My boss's boss was telling me this over coffee one afternoon. It was the first quarter that we'd missed our numbers after years of exceeding them. But now a competitor was eating our lunch by beating us at hospital contracting one account at a time. Things were looking bad. Over the next few months, one senior leader after another would leave the company: voluntarily and involuntarily. I still have a lot of friends who work there, but it took the business unit years to get back on track.

I should have left when I saw the warning signs, but I made the mistake of believing them. They continually promised if we stayed on board, there would be 'great opportunities' to grow our career, do new things, and benefit from this turnaround. None of that was true. Two more rounds of layoffs later, budgets were slashed so much you couldn't get your work done, which resulted in missing your mid-year and annual review objectives. Promotions that were promised were rescinded, job scopes and responsibilities were changed without warning, and the general morale was so bad— even Mr. Rogers would have a hard time staying positive.

When companies reach the end phase of their life cycle, many people get tricked into thinking it's an opportunity. An opportunity to contribute or be part of the turn-around or an opportunity to watch attrition and capitalize on it by getting a promotion. And companies are directly responsible for this mistaken assumption. They actively tell employees they will be a critical piece of the turnaround process, and they have become indispensable. The truth is when the company says that 'they need you more than ever,' the rule of getting more out of your company than they do out of you becomes impossible.

As the company turns the corner from success to managing failure, there is a playbook they generally follow that will ultimately serve them and not you. I've seen this playbook play out twice in my career, twice in my wife's, and countless times in the careers of friends. I call this the "Dying Business Playbook."

Know The "Dying Business Playbook"

What are some of the specific things you should look for that could unexpectedly trick you into blindly committing to a failing company against your best interest? Before we get into the "playbook," every failing business gives off warning signs in advance. Here are some early indicators that should tell you it may be time to make sure your life raft and personal floatation devices are in order.

For instance, budget cuts aren't a warning sign in and of themselves, but if they start occurring every quarter or if you have a surprisingly deep cut, then this would be an indication. Also major priority shifts such as large projects becoming unfunded, or when important projects from the beginning of the year mysteriously become unimportant. If there's a senior staff shake-up—when you notice older, tenured, staff leaving suddenly—that's another one. The veterans know the signs and know not to play this game. These are the warning signs to watch out for that usually foreshadow the more obvious spending freezes, travel restrictions, and payment term extensions: your business is headed for troubled waters!

When a business gets to this point, where they have to make such radical changes—lock down travel, slash budgets, cancel projects, eliminate lunches during noon meetings, disappearing "free" coffee—when those things happen, know that it's not going to be fixed easily or quickly. You're in for a really long haul. If you've somehow missed, or ignored, the early warning signs, the next step of the playbook will kick in shortly after this. I call this Phase II, and it's marked by hellish hiring freezes, lame layoffs, and eerily empty desks.

This is War

"If you aren't 110% in, then we don't want you here. This is a war, and we need to know who is on our side."

The clearest sign of trouble is when leadership begins to talk about the situation in terms of 'war.' When people talk about competitive situations as 'wars' there is a mindset shift that occurs within the organization and within the thinking the people at the company. When things are deemed as 'wars,' it reduces the ethics individuals or companies are willing to adhere to. Suddenly it's a life and death situation. It throws off everyone's sensitivities to what is right and wrong and puts team members in a defensive position where they will justify behaviors that wouldn't otherwise be appropriate.

Once the 'war' has been established, step one of the playbook involves restricting travel and entertainment. The company is watching their bottom line closely. Travel is the easiest thing to control and manage and allows the company to reduce expenses with minimal short term problems. Restricting the ability for staff to travel or even entertain customers begins the shift from a long term outlook to a short term outlook. The company is now in survival mode.

The next step is belt-tightening. This happens once the company's leadership is able to look at the situation with more time to reflect on it. Often you will hear phrases like 'do more with less' or 'we have to tighten our belts.' You will see middle managers get almost giddy when they find ways to save money or cut expected expenses because they are looking for the short term rewards they think the company will give them. These phrases are another signal that resources will be increasingly limited. This means it will be harder for you to accomplish your own skill development. Remember that our goal is to ensure you are developing skills so you are more valuable to yourself than to the company, and your options increase. If you don't have the budget to do those projects that allow you to learn, then you can't develop the new skills.

"Activity Metrics" and Other Clever Distractions

The next thing you will see is a shift to an interest in activity. When leadership is pressured to explain why things aren't happening and explain how the situation will be turned around, the focus quickly becomes about what everyone is doing to make things better. Results take a backseat to activity. You will see activity metrics, and the requirement will be an increase in action. They won't focus on the validity of those actions, but rather will want to evaluate what and how much is being done. This is because leadership too is trying to 'manage up' and wants to appear like they are doing everything they can to get the results that they so desperately need.

Management may take a second look at the approved current business plans and ask for a reevaluation of them. What they want is to pressure test the strategic and tactical plans and see if they can find projects or programs that don't have a really good rationale. They will request changes that will likely move you away from mid or long term solutions to fixing short term issues and drive up activity, matching the new activity-based mentality.

Leadership wants to be seen as taking action, and the result will drive a new mentality throughout the organization, one that values activity over thinking. As the old plans become new plans, you will see a drive towards increasingly unrealistic expectations. These unrealistic expectations will be very frustrating in light of the new budget restrictions. The natural reaction will be to double down on a high activity culture because it will become clear that sometimes the only resources left are the grunts who haven't left for a better job.

Low-value work that used to be outsourced will show up on your plate because you will be the only one left to do it. A focus on doing activities that don't fix the real problem will stand in the way of achieving your goals. But your goals don't matter to leadership. They have to follow the playbook. Going against it puts them personally at risk as they are now fighting for their jobs. The difference between them and you? They know they are fighting for their jobs, they are only fooling you into thinking you aren't.

Hours Go Up as Businesses Go Down

What impact does this have on the staff when the 'save the business' playbook is implemented? The most substantial and imminent impact is that work hours will go up. To 'save the business' you will see a natural inclination to make people more productive. It will come out as an invisible pressure you feel from all around you. You will see your co-workers working more without being asked. For instance, after one 'belt tightening' meeting where it was clear we were in "save the business" mode, 90% of the staff banded together and decided everyone should be working until 6pm. You will see managers roaming the halls at 5:30 quietly noting who is there and who isn't. You will feel a pressure to stay longer and longer even if your work is already done for the day.

The highly talented are the ones that get hurt by this the most. Somehow, the staff that are mediocre, always feel this change and begin looking for new roles elsewhere. The extra work and pressure affect them the most, and they can't hide like they used to. Like rats fleeing a sinking ship, these people will leave the company or business, and you will see large scale attrition. In nearly all situations, the vacated roles don't get filled, and work is distributed to whoever is left. Leadership, managing the P&L, look at it as an opportunity to improve the bottom line, and sometimes see it as a gift.

Great leaders use the opportunity to evaluate the workload and will eliminate activities that are not value-added. Unfortunately, great leaders like this are rare, and you most often see a general redistribution of the work. As the long hours begin to pile up more and more, coworkers will give off more and more dramatic behaviors. The pressure and stress will take its toll on the everyone coming in, contributing, and burning the midnight oil on work instead of spending time with their families. Blowups, arguments, disagreements, and misunderstandings will become commonplace and frequent. Gossip will be rampant. Critical team members you may rely on to get things done that were reliable become difficult and unpredictable. Work friends become distant.

Franken-Job – Disaster "New Roles" During a Downturn

This is the point where loyal, high potential employees get tricked into thinking there will be opportunities for them. The truth is, career progression in these situations becomes wildly unpredictable. While occasionally you will see advancement and opportunities open up, it typically is the result of vacated positions you find have been neglected by the previous occupant who carved out time to find a new job by ignoring their current one.

Very often the promotions come through the combination of two old roles into one, without the support system to be successful in the new "Frankenstein" position. This exact thing has happened to me twice. My old, full-time role was scaled up to include someone else's vacated full-time role at the same time that attrition had reduced the staff reporting to me to a skeleton crew. Sometimes the title won't even be adjusted to reflect the new role, and the pay increases will be limited, if any at all, accompanied with leaders saying things like, "We're lucky to have jobs at all!"

Each one of these 'opportunities' is a shining mirage, and just like an illusion, career plans and commitments evaporate without warning. Promotions that once were right around the corner are frozen by managers and leaders continually moving the goal post down the field. I've had two great staff members reporting to me been bitten in the ass by this.

One employee—let's call her Elizabeth—had a defined performance plan with benchmarks that, once achieved, would result in their promotion—but it didn't happen. She jumped through hoops to do everything that was asked of her only to find that once she achieved the benchmarks, new goals and development were added that weren't part of the original deal. Elizabeth had no recourse. They were in complete control, and they applied "subjective considerations" to weasel out of granting her the promotion she bent over backward to make happen.

Elizabeth's story isn't unique, and companies employ other shady tactics including freezing annual raises, reducing bonus target achievements, or trying to pass off your annual raise as additional compensation for taking on significantly more work in your role.

The other chapters in this book are much more about tactics you can employ to get the most out of your experience at a company and provide value that helps you continue to get more and more skills and expertise. This chapter is different in that the only action you need to do is to recognize when a company turns the corner from good to bad, and don't get fooled. The only solution is to leave for another opportunity as fast as you can.

Of course, the company will try to get you to commit even further, but as I've talked to others and looked back at each one of my experiences, there isn't one person who benefited fully from 'riding it out.' Even the ones who grew in their role or were promoted noted the heavy emotional toll it took and recognized if they had left, they would have been better off. Of course, some will say they never would have gotten to the level they are at without sticking it out. Maybe that's true. But I'll bet those people were low performers with low potential (We know that's not you, so don't fall into that trap).

Don't Wear Out Your Welcome

"Do you remember a dinner you had with customers in Ojai California? You were at a resort, and it looks like there were about fifteen surgeons there," The lawyer said. I had made the mistake of trying to ride out the downturn, and there I was sitting in a room with HR and the legal team, as they reviewed my old expense reports. Our company was under intense DOJ scrutiny, and it seemed like every other week I was getting dragged in front of the 'kangaroo court' for evaluation.

"Refresh my memory," I responded. She told me that the meeting had occurred five years earlier and was at a cardiac conference with surgeons.

Of course, I remembered that meeting. I remember them all. But I'd learned to never tell them anything they didn't specifically ask about. And regardless, it was so long ago, there was no reason to trust my memory on specifics until I knew what they were getting at. She was asking me to recollect one dinner out of approximately 125 that I had conducted over that period of time. She began asking me extremely specific questions about the business purpose for the meeting, what was discussed, who was in attendance, even down to the amount and types of wine that were ordered that evening.

As I walked them through what I recalled from the meeting, they started to identify things at that dinner that they claimed were violations of policy. But oddly, not violations of the current policy when the dinner had occurred, but rather violations of the *new* policies that they had created years later.

They continued to pick apart all of my past business and personnel decisions and hold me to a different standard than what was in place at the time. I was dumbfounded. I learned a valuable lesson that day: staying in one business unit can result in a variety of negative things for you personally. Regardless of whether the company is a sinking ship, staying with one group for more than three to four years creates a situation where you become pigeonholed, scrutinized for previous decisions, and your actions held against policy changes that at the time were unforeseeable.

The reason why you want to move business groups every three to four years is to avoid the impact of your mistakes. In other words, don't wait for the bill to come. You will be expected to fix the mistakes you've made, and in that situation, you are not learning new skills, just reinforcing old ones.

Many people will claim that it's good to see the impact of your decisions over time and see how they play out. Unfortunately, the impact on your career if you do this is likely to be detrimental. One issue with this is you can't ignore or avoid these problems because it's obvious that these are problems you created.

Even if you've moved on into another part of the same business unit, another project, or another brand, you will always be pulled back in to help fix the problems. The difficulty in facing problems you've created and trying to solve them is that people will want a new and creative idea that is harder to execute than if you started from scratch. These are things you want to avoid because when you are in a mental space of higher learning, you want the ability and freedom to fail fast and not have mistakes hanging over your head.

Staying in a group more than three to four years can also result in wearing out your welcome. Have you ever had a party at your home and had a guest stay well after everyone else had left? Can you remember how tiresome their personality became the longer they stayed? If you spend too long working with the same people, this could be you. Unfortunately, familiarity breeds contempt. Also, what I have found is that high performers have a drive and often a personality focused on achievement that many others find annoying over time. You could be seen as combative, crass, arrogant, or condescending. As time goes by it's harder to keep these personality traits under wraps, and harder for those you work with to be accepting of every part of you.

As people understand your strengths and weaknesses, they will exploit your faults or point out your mistakes to others. This is a dangerous situation and one that makes it harder and harder to be a high achiever year after year. People learn about your family and your personal choices and begin to see when and how you trade-off between work and home. Irritation and jealousy ensue.

Additionally, if you are a team leader, it will get harder and harder to motivate a team using the same methods and tricks. Your team members who have worked with you very closely will begin to be increasingly annoyed at how you approach problems. Once they think they have seen it all, they will begin to think they can do your job just as well as you can.

Over time, they will begin to see you as the flawed individual you are, rather than looking up to you as a leader. This makes it significantly harder to motivate them and keep them engaged. Ultimately, what you want is a team that is highly motivated and believes in you as a leader, so they are excited to help you and take work off your plate, which will free you up for new skill development and career exploration.

Once you've moved on, your old tried-and-true tested ideas will seem like new innovative solutions to problems.
This will position you to look like you're making better decisions, solving problems faster than your colleagues, and should (hopefully) impress your leaders and stakeholders.

TAKE HOME LESSONS:
- When the company says 'they need you more than ever' and there are going to be opportunities that arise from 'helping us turn it around' it is a clear signal that the remainder of your time there will be very challenging.

- Companies follow a playbook when they start missing numbers. They implement a war mentality which results in throwing out their old culture and replacing it with a 'whatever is necessary' culture.
- Budgets are slashed, travel is restricted, the activity becomes more important than results. Attrition begins, backfills don't happen, and workload gets spread to those that are left, resulting in more hours worked and less choices to build skills.
- While the company will employ a variety of tactics to keep you, your progress can be stunted significantly, and you should aggressively find a new job.
- Even if the company isn't going down, staying in one group lowers your earnings and learnings, skill set development, and can pigeonhole you.
- Moving every three to four years ensures you avoid the impact of any mistakes you make, ensures you don't wear out your welcome and allows you to use tried and true tested frameworks to appear as a rapid and creative problem solver.

ACTION ITEM:

Update your resume to a current version that reflects your greatest experiences and is easy to update when (not if, but when) your company takes a turn for the worse. By reading this book, you may discover that even if your company hasn't taken a turn for the worse, you would be better off honing and building your skills somewhere else that isn't a disaster.

CHAPTER X
YOU CAN'T FIX A BAD BOSS...SO DON'T BOTHER

Jim had been at his job for a few years when he got a new boss named Charles. Charles was a Senior Director that took over for a boss that everyone loved. At first, things looked very hopeful. When Charles came in, he said all the right things: "I have three kids, and family is the most important thing," and "Growth and development is so important...let's get you into this emerging leaders program!" But within about two months, Jim realized none of this was true, Charles was just blowing smoke up everyone's ass to make them think he was a good boss.

Very soon, Jim realized that Charles' poor management skills were clashing with his ability to be successful or advance his career. Jim wasn't a new manager, he had years of experience. But Charles, regardless of experience, managed everyone as if they were inferior. Charles second guessed Jim's decisions and asked for revisions over and over. You couldn't predict the complaints; one week he'd want it one way and the next, the exact opposite. Every conference call, Charles would denigrate the other men's ideas, but always agreed to the female team member's suggestions. Charles expected you to jump at a moment's notice, too: vacations, holidays, weekends, weddings, it didn't matter. And if you didn't reply right away, he would continuously hound you until you broke down and answered. A single unanswered text from Charles could get you a slew of voicemails and texts—in ALL CAPS!

Jim began having panic attacks and second-guessing himself. He lost his confidence. About twice a year, on the verge of a breakdown, he would work up the nerve to confront Charles, then disappear for a week and refuse to turn on his phone. Charles would tiptoe around Jim for about a month and start back up again...continuing the cycle of abuse and even upping the ante by being even worse than before. It was his way of reinforcing that you better just keep quiet. Eventually, Jim gave up fighting back entirely.

This might sound familiar to you. There's a reason why bad bosses act this way, and it has to do with their insecurities. Because they are so intensely insecure, they secretly believe they could get fired at any time. This causes them to become 'yes men' that are at the immediate disposal of THEIR boss. It isn't about managing down at all, it's all about managing up. They will do their boss's bidding, and no matter how ridiculous or unrealistic the request, and they never say no. Because they have this mentality with their boss, they expect the same of you. As a result, their impossible expectations trickle down onto you. They expect you to drop everything at a moment's notice. They act unpredictability. They can't take feedback. They don't care about others. And because this is all stemming from insecurity...you cannot EVER change a bad boss.

So where is Jim now? Jim's company had layoffs, and Charles targeted the team members who weren't doing exactly as they were told. Unfortunately, Jim wasn't one of them. He still works for Charles. He never sees his kids and is at Charles's beck and call. Even worse, when I ask Jim when he's going to find a new job, he says, "This is the best job I'll be able to get. If I went somewhere else, I'd have to take a pay cut." Jim's confidence has been shattered. He's given up on his career.

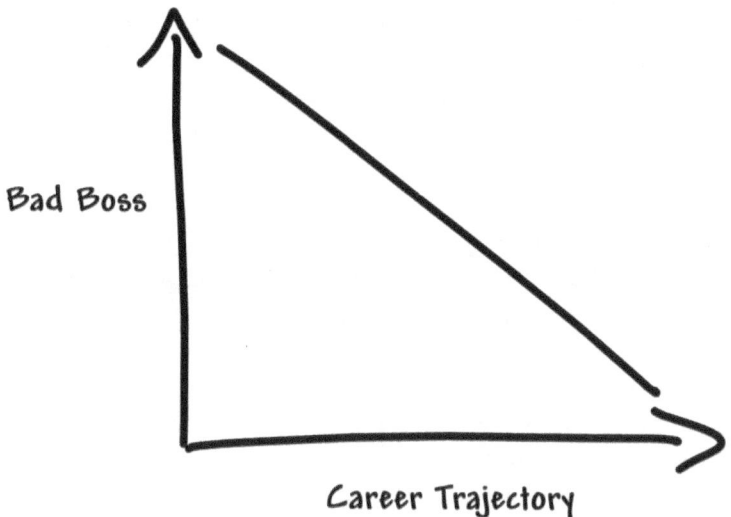

Countless times I've seen the effect bad bosses have on coworkers, friends, and loved ones. At first, the well-meaning employee will try to modify their behavior to appease the bad boss. They think, *if I could only give them exactly what they ask for, maybe that will work. If I make myself more available, maybe that will change them*. This is erroneous thinking. YOU'LL NEVER FIX A BAD BOSS. They will only stall your career, demoralize you, and make every day miserable. They'll encroach on your weekends, ruin your vacations, destroy your family time, and create a never ending experience of anxiety. I cannot stress this enough, if you encounter one of these terrible individuals, find a new role, or find a way out of their group as quickly as you can.

But first, before you run out and find a new job, you should diagnose the situation. Do you *truly* have a bad boss?

What are the qualities to look for in a boss to determine if they qualify as bad enough to begin exploring other opportunities? There are four categories of what a boss does to become a <u>bad</u> boss. While inexperience will result in sloppy management, generally those aren't behaviors driven by insecurity. It's the *insecure* bosses that create serious issues with colleagues or direct reports. To help you diagnose how bad your boss's insecurities may be, there are four types of behaviors bad bosses routinely do: they create anxiety, they inhibit your success, they act illogically and shady. But remember, a bad boss doesn't do these things once or twice. You're looking for every day, every week, every project type of behavior.

To help you identify them better, I've broken them down into archetypes.

The Neurotic

This type of bad boss will create anxiety by completely breaking boundaries. They are so insecure they are like that ex that cannot stop obsessing over you. A neurotic Boss will totally ignore any need you might have for downtime on the evenings, weekends, holidays, and vacations. They will routinely ask for things over the weekends or holidays. They will frantically email you and text you on a holiday— I've even seen weddings and infringed honeymoons (such as mine). As they continually ask you for information and expect speedy responses while you are busy doing other things, the anxiety starts to build. Text messages or emails sit unanswered, just waiting for a response. And they keep coming in. DING...DING...DING.

This type of boss doesn't respect your marriage or care about how not being around may affect your relationship with your family or spouse. If you don't prioritize work over your family commitments, this "Stage Five Clinger" will imply you are at risk of failing in your job or worse.

Their continued interruption into your home life drives the overall anxiety up because you aren't ever able to get away, relax, and disconnect. They are so bad at controlling their own natural anxiety and neuroticism that they can't disconnect themselves from others. Their need for control results in their continued disruption of your private life. No matter how organized and effective you are, they will disrupt your flow, resulting in a reduction in your ability to learn and succeed.

The Career Assassin

Bad bosses inhibit your success, and they do it in several ways. A "Career Assassin" will micromanage you and second guess your every choice, not allowing you to develop decision-making skills. They'll tie up all your time by inviting you to a barrage of meetings and conference calls so you can't get work done unless you are at home. They will constantly set expectations and then move the bar higher so they are impossible to meet. They aren't doing this intentionally, necessarily. This constant change in direction is indicative of their insecurity in their own decision making and results in an inability to stick to any one course of action without constant changes.

As this career saboteur directs you to do this or that, they will naturally want to keep you in a box and restrict you to a limited set of activities. When you try to build new skills, they will get frustrated and migrate you back to the old activities. This is because the development of new skills threatens them. You might actually leave, or know something they don't.

As a last resort, when they feel their control over you slipping away, they will get very angry. Especially if they learn you are exploring other career options. This is particularly difficult if you are looking internally within the same company. They will potentially sabotage your chances with another group to keep you under their thumb, so they don't have to break in a new employee who is a wild card. They have a habit of sharing poor feedback about you to others because you aren't making them happy. These other potential bosses don't know that your boss is impossible to please, so this will look bad for you. Work hard to protect yourself as you job hunt, or you can end up with no options to move to another group and a bad boss that becomes vindictive.

The Chaos Maker

Bad bosses are great at being very illogical. The "Chaos Maker" seems to operate on a level of nonsense making that defies all logic. If you have this type of boss, you'll be tearing your hair out trying to accommodate their fanciful tactics. They simply don't have a thought process to evaluate problems objectively and come up with solutions effectively. They can't see the logic in plans that are well laid out and will make very subjective changes. In addition to their general instability, they are too easily persuaded by others— but even if left to their own devices they would inevitably change directions later, or forget they agreed in the first place.

Beware, this type of boss also isn't able to take feedback. If you confront your "Mad Hatter," of a boss, you may get excuses, apologies, and sincere promises to do better— only to find the very next day they've gone back on their word.

The Shady Character

Bad bosses are shady. The "Shady Character" is the master at manipulating people into doing what they want, or doing things that aren't in their best interest. They will tell you they want honesty and use your words against you. They will tell you things are good for your career when they really aren't. And if you try to go in a different direction, they will guilt you for not doing exactly what they told you to do.

When Shady Characters make mistakes, they will shirk any accountability for it. They will play the blame game and shift responsibility to other people. Sometimes they will assign blame to the nearest person. In the same light, they will always attempt to undermine you with business partners or customers. I've routinely seen shady bosses 'check-up' on employees with customers in secret. If the customer makes any kind of negative feedback, instead of being supportive, the Shady Character will throw you under the bus, and use it against you in performance reviews or during check-in meetings. SURPRISE! This tactic is designed to keep you off balance and always feeling as if you aren't performing effectively so you will work even harder at trying to make them happy.

Worst of all, the Shady Character will steal your ideas. They will use all kinds of mental gymnastics to justify it. They will even convince themselves that they didn't take your idea, but rather, they were the ones to plant a seedling of an idea in your head, and you ran with it. They'll convince themselves that they were the real difference maker and that they were simply building something greater off a small, inconsequential thing you said. If it weren't for them, nothing would exist at all!

The hardest part is when a bad boss takes your idea because it's impossible to undo it. You look like you aren't a team player if you accuse them of stealing it, and even worse, you'll put yourself at risk with your boss if you call them out on it. As hard as it is, if your boss takes one of your ideas, swallow your pride and move on. But take the lesson to heart, use it as another confirmation they are a bad boss. And another reason why you are planning to get out.

You Have a Bad Boss...So Now What?

I've found, in good companies and bad, you'll run into legitimately narcissistic personality types in positions of power. Finding one of these isn't necessarily an indication that your company is a bad one. These types of people escape detection, and it happens in companies most of the time just by accident. Maybe they had a bad screening processes, or they've been promoting people too quickly. More than a few bad bosses in one organization may be indicative of it being not a very mature company. But honestly, bad bosses can be found anywhere. Even in great companies.

Now that you've diagnosed the situation and have decided you do truly have a bad boss, what do you do about it? We already determined it's because the root of the problem is this person's insecurity, and you've learned you're not going to be able to fix a bad boss. You aren't going to change them, and no amount of feedback is going to sink in or cause them to act differently. Make no mistake if you have determined you have a bad boss
your only solution is to leave the role, so you are no longer reporting to or working with this person. There is no middle ground. A person who has a number of the qualities mentioned above cannot be changed, and will only negatively affect your career and your stress levels. Number one goal is to leave and find another job.

Beware of false hope. During the course of your search, you will be fooled at times into thinking that things have changed. Your bad boss will occasionally act like a normal boss. They will show signs that they are changing. They'll recognize you for doing good work, praise you in front of colleagues, or mysteriously stop micromanaging you for a few weeks. But fundamentally he or she will always backtrack into their normal behavior pattern of being a bad boss. Having a bad boss is like having a bad back, the symptoms come and go. Sometimes you feel great, but when the pain comes back, you're absolutely miserable.

My advice is to get organized, start your new job search, and make sure you're managing your search in a way that prioritizes finding a job above everything else, so you don't get suckered into a false sense of security. While you're engaged in a job search, there are some additional strategies that can help you minimize your boss's overreaction and overall bad behaviors. These aren't long term solutions. These tactics are *short-term tactics* that can only be used for a limited amount of time because they will eventually catch up to you! They are only designed to make your job as tolerable as possible in the context of having a bad boss, but they could come back to harm you if you ended up not committing to finding a new job, or were somehow tricked you into thinking the bad boss it changed their ways.

Flattery Bomb

The first tactic you should use on your bad boss is to shamelessly compliment them. The reason a bad boss is so bad is because they are either intensely insecure or they are an egomaniac. Because of that, constantly complimenting them will help reduce their targeted attacks on you, and will focus them on someone else who is not as complimentary. You'll have to make sure your compliment appears sincere, and that they don't think you are doing it only to their face. Instead of complimenting them in a general way, compliment them on ways that they are helping you, such as teaching you new things, setting you up for success, or giving you an opportunity. This will still stroke their ego because it's not solely focused on them, so they won't automatically interpret your compliment as sucking up.

Stay on Message

The second short-term tactic is to tell them what they want to hear. This one is tricky because if you just tell them what they want to hear and there is nothing to back it up, it will backfire. Make sure when you're telling them what they want to hear it is always around topics that are subjective, such as your opinion about work, or your thoughts about how a problem should be tackled. This way it's harder to be proven wrong, and you aren't just giving them ammo they can use against you.

Telling them what they want to hear means telling them how much effort you are putting into solving the problem you're working on, instead of talking about the result you expect. Even more important is to tell them how you are solving it exactly how they directed you to solve it. This way, they feel you're following their advice because you believe it is for the best — which will also stroke their ego and reduce their insecurity.

The Sidestep

Trick number three is to resist the urge to confront your bad boss or give them any feedback based on reality. They will ask for it, with their personal insecurity driving their curiosity. There is a small part of themselves that thinks they can handle the feedback. They can't! They may ask you questions like 'what can I do to help you more' or 'what can I do differently' or 'what could I do better?' When you hear these statements, you should immediately go on high alert! These questions will lull you into responding with honesty. Reference the 'Never tell the truth' chapter to remind you why this is a BAD idea. The bad boss won't be comfortable with you answering 'nothing.' You will have to give them something. And here is where the Sidestep comes into play.

Topics to avoid talking about with your bad boss are: clashing working styles, excessive micromanaging, undermining, stealing your ideas or taking credit for your work, blame game or any gas-lighting they do. Instead, tell them complimentary things. Pick out things they do that help you, even if they are minor. This will temporarily satisfy the itch to tell them what they can do better. Treat this like you do a job interview. When interviewers ask you 'what is your greatest weakness,' we all know to answer things like, 'I work too hard' or 'I'm too committed to my work.' This is the same type of question. So, when they push you to answer, you have to say things like, "I would love to hear more insights about the state of the business," or "I'd love more coaching on how to get where you are one day," or "I'd love advice on how to [insert skill here that they don't have]."

If you have a bad boss, they won't actually be interested in investing in you. And because of that, these pieces of feedback are completely innocuous and put the ball in their court to do something with. They aren't offensiv, and over the long term, WHEN you leave, you will be able to use them as reasons and validations for why you are moving on, if pressed. The point is, be prepared. They will ask this question, and you have to be ready to answer. Have these responses in your back pocket.

Bite the Bullet

The fourth trick is to bite the bullet and do their dirty work. Don't argue with them when they ask you to do menial tasks (so they don't have to do them). When you push back, bad bosses can get very angry. Their insecurity and egotism will overrule any logic and they will interpret it as you being insubordinate or will perceive you as a threat because you feel certain work is below you. While doing these menial tasks, it can be very frustrating because it is inhibiting you from moving forward in your career. It should be clear at this point, and should only reinforce that you must leave the situation.

TAKE HOME LESSONS:
- You will not change a bad boss. Bad bosses only hurt or stall your career.
- If you determine you are working for one you must find a new role as rapidly as possible.

- Bad bosses hurt you in three distinct ways: they create anxiety, they inhibit your success, and they undermine you.
- If you have confirmed you have a bad boss, there is an action plan: find a new job. Until you've found a new position, use short term tactics to make your job tolerable.

ACTION ITEM:
Write out four pieces of innocuous feedback you can give your bad boss when they ask for your opinion about how they are doing and how they can help you more than they are today.

CHAPTER XI
YOUR BRAND IS MORE IMPORTANT THAN YOUR COMPANY'S

Each chapter leading up to now has been establishing the foundation for you to create the greatest ally to your career, but your worst enemy if you ignore it: your personal brand.

Your personal brand is your professional identity. A consistent set of facts about you that you present and is accepted by others. Curated with intention, it can serve you well. But if you allow others to create your personal brand for you, it can be the single greatest factor that holds you back in your career. Developing and owning your personal brand can guarantee you're working on projects you love, but when someone else defines it for you, it can force you into a never-ending cycle of projects you hate.

Let me give you an example.

Remember how I made the choice to join a company at a lower level role to learn a different side of my industry? This job was way more tactical than I ever could have anticipated. Within three months, I knew it wasn't a good fit for me, but I was tied down after signing a signing and retention bonus. So, I decided to take the opportunity to get an experience that few people in my industry get: seeing their customers from the inside. So, instead of pulling myself down into a tactician role and lowering my value, I bucked the system and consistently worked on projecting a unique personal brand within my department, that of a master strategist.

I deliberately took a step back from the day to day requirements of the job and began thinking with a long-term outlook. My colleagues were in the weeds, and I was in the clouds. From a 30,000 foot view, I looked at what skills the department and the overall company seemed to be lacking. I noticed there were tons of people who were great at creative, great at reading books and regurgitating what others had written, or great at 'getting tactical,' but very few were thinking with the end in mind, developing a plan, or coming up with their own ideas. I knew I had to avoid being a clone. So, I worked hard to create a personal brand to differentiate myself from others based on what was missing. I positioned myself as forward-thinking, authentic and honest, strategic, innovative, a change agent, and maybe even a bit ballsy.

Colleagues warned me, "This could burn you, this sort of thing makes leadership uncomfortable."

I worked hard to develop relationships with key influencers who saw my value within the organization (as I described in Rule Bender Five). Eventually, the day came. My boss—the nicest guy in the world—came to me and said, "I need someone who loves creative development in this department, and we know that's not what you love." I sat there quietly, awaiting the details. He said, "We know you can provide the greatest value doing enterprise strategy. They need help solving the biggest problems the organization has, so we want you to do that full time."

I barely contained a fist pump as I thought, *"Win, win." They can take the foundation I built here and execute on it, and I can go up and work on longer term, tougher problems, and add something very unique to my resume and list of accomplishments.* It was a better fit for me, matched my skills and what I love to do, and the move would allow me to work with people who need difficult problem solving and radical solutions, rather than people who seemed to want clone like behavior. But this redirect never would have happened if I hadn't created and lived my personal brand of being a high-level strategic thinker—and put my brand above all else.

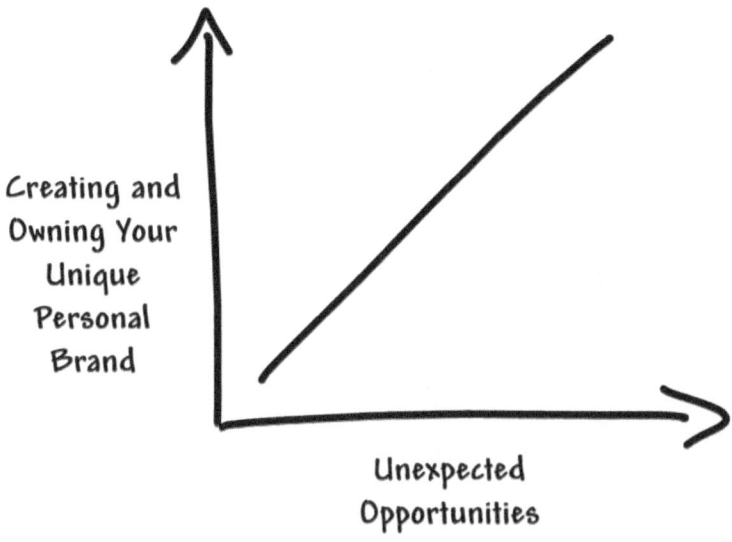

Because of my deeper business and professional experiences and the sheer fact that I'm confident enough not to worry about losing my job— I'm comfortable that I'll find another one— I was able to not second guess my personal strategy. Once I was there, I started painting my personal brand as a big strategic thinker that wasn't going to get bogged down in details. But I also knew that I couldn't just go in there and throw up crappy plans. I had to deliver clear and impactful strategic thinking at a high level. Eventually, they ran out of tough problems for me to solve. It won't work if you're just faking it, so tailor your personal brand to your greatest strengths that differentiate you.

Your personal brand is like your aura. It's what attracts you to what you really want in your career, and repels the things you don't. Don't over-engineer it. Create a personal brand from the values you live by, cultivate it, and express it as part of you. You're bringing what you want into your life, you're in charge, and it also places you in the mindset of what your future identity is. When you're actively living inside your personal brand, it will become immediately clear to you—and to everyone around you—when you're in a job that isn't a good fit, and it will propel you forward into a position you're suitable for.

If I could roll back my career fifteen years, there is a lot I would do differently. It took me years to figure out that you should be curating what you want out of your career and establishing your brand proactively, instead of allowing others to label you. You're not supposed to let other people decide what your life should look like. If you let that happen, they'll end up saying things like, "You're really good at cleaning up the break room!" Or, "You're great at flyers!" You have to take the bull by the horns, and attract higher level projects and positions that you want. But this requires a conscious effort to guide your coworkers towards a thoughtfully created and owned brand that showcases your skills and strengths, while simultaneously rejecting things that dilute your value.

Don't Dilute Your Value

Personal branding is about establishing control over your career, building the skill sets you want to build, doing work you are the best at and enjoy the most, and avoiding the work you hate. People naturally feel that they should be well rounded so they are seen as flexible and able to do a variety of things. They feel like if they hedge and are good at a number of different skills, then they will always have a job. What they don't realize is that by doing this, they are diluting their value.

Personal branding is not just about the things you want to do— it's about protecting yourself from the things you *don't* want to do. You can't count on anyone else to tell your story within the organization. It's not your boss's job, it's not your coworkers' job, it's not human resource's job...it's your job. And you need to make sure you build in time and allocate the effort to do it.

So, let's get tactical...what is your personal brand? It's your personal elevator pitch. Your personal brand builds from your strengths, not your weaknesses. It allows you to define who you want to be and help to avoid who you don't want to be. Your personal brand helps you articulate who you decide to help, what problem you solve, and what value you provide to those you work for or with. You bring value to any given situation. Your personal brand helps you convey your value in skills you bring as a result of carefully analyzing and choosing what you're best at. It's the Yin and the Yang of what you want to highlight.

So how do you develop your personal brand? The first thing to do is to sit down and list out all of the qualities, characteristics, skills, and experiences you have accumulated to this day. Take those and distill them down into the common themes you enjoy focusing on. I'm a believer that you'll get much more out of your own personal strengths than trying to fix your weaknesses. (Even Gallup agrees with this in their Strength Finders data and book.) So, during this process, make sure you are focusing on the things that come naturally or easy to you. Taking the skills that come easily to you and then focusing on projects that use them is critically important to managing your success. This helps you control your day-to-day work life and ensures you're successful and happy.

When developed correctly, this will tee you up for projects and roles you love, allowing you to be successful, while simultaneously keeping you away from things you hate or aren't that good at. By defining your brand strategically, it will help you get deployed to specific business problems that appear to be too difficult or ill-suited for others. You want to, and can create a situation where you are the go-to resource for your favorite types of projects. When you have a high-value personal brand, you can be choosier about what you work on and will have the ability to push back on your leadership and force them to make choices about where best to use you.

Most people let others establish the narrative rather than taking control of it. This is a very critical differentiation between people who get control of their careers and those who don't. The person who has control of their career is constantly establishing and reinforcing their own personal brand. They will be thoughtful about creating it, and also diligent about getting the message across the organization as if they were a product (which in fact you are). Assuming you are able to create your brand around valuable skills or characteristics, you can then begin to establish yourself as a thought leader internally within the organization and in your industry at large.

Once you have the list of 8 to 10 different skills and qualities, you need to rank them. Ranking them is a subjective exercise, and you should consider a few things. Make sure you are taking into account how good you are at the skill or quality, how much you like to use that skill or quality, how different it makes you from other people that would be considered your peers or one level up, and the overall value that skill or quality brings to the organization.

Skill Weighting System	Value	Aptitude	Differentiation	Love	Score
Skill 1	Value 1				
Skill 2	Value 2				
Skill 3	Value 3				
Skill 4	Value 4				
Skill 5	Value 5				
Force Rank Each Skill / Value 1-10 for each category					

Your Personal Brand Statement

After you have sorted and ranked the skills, it is time to develop your personal brand statement. This is the manifesto you use as your North Star, to both help guide you in your day-to-day actions, as well as tell your story within your organization. You will have to decide how customized you want this statement to be in relation to your current organization, or if you want to try to make a broader statement that you can use externally as well. There's an easy framework you can use to develop your personal brand statement. Break it up into three sections:
The thing you do,
How you do it (describing the important skills you evaluated),
And the value it brings.

Here are some examples:
I'm great at problem solving and action planning. I help grow businesses by rapidly assessing the opportunities and challenges they face and building an easy to execute plan so they can grow faster.
I'm great at understanding customer motivations and how to affect behavioral change. I help customers adopt our services by creating marketing materials that speak to them emotionally, so they are more interested.
I'm great at budgeting and finance and project planning. I help our internal business units by giving them advice on how to manage their budgets to get the greatest value out of their dollar.

Your Personal Avoidance Statement

You should also develop your personal avoidance statement. This is a similar exercise to the personal brand statement, but it is designed to help you consistently explain what you're *not* good at or want to avoid in your role. This also can be broken into three sections:

I'm not much help on this (whatever project or task you'd like to avoid), but I could add a lot of insight to this other thing (another way of providing value), which is how I can add more value.

Go through the exercise of writing down the 8 to 10 skills, qualities, or characteristics you want to minimize or avoid. Similarly, as in the exercise about your greatest skills, you will want to use subjective factors as well. What skills do other people seem to have across your peer group? In trying to create your own personal brand, as well as the things you want to avoid, you're looking for things that make you stand out. Skills, characteristics, or qualities that everyone else demonstrates may be an important part of your avoidance statement to ensure you aren't just another clone getting lost in the crowd.

Here are some examples:

I won't be much help determining whether creative visuals impact the customers. But once you have, I will be able to make sure we have the tools to really impact the customer, which is the most important thing.

I'm not great at searching to find a way to save 10% on this small contract. But what I can do is push the agency for better quality work by giving them more direction, which creates a better value.
I won't be much help defining a process to make that better. But when you get it, I'll be great at making sure the entire team understands it and follows it, which is really what will make the difference.

Promote Your Personal Brand

Once you've developed your personal brand statement and your avoidance statement, you have to create your engagement strategy. If people don't know about you and your personal brand, then the "story" you've created isn't worth anything. You have to determine your engagement points to tell your story, and you need to look at normal day-to-day interactions differently than you used to. Each interaction you have, whether it be a meeting, time in the elevator, milling around with colleagues waiting for a conference room to open up, walking out of the building to get lunch, or walking to your car after a long day— are all opportunities for you to tell your story to others. But to maximize this opportunity, you have to practice both of the statements, so they roll off the tongue naturally when the opportunity presents itself.

Handling Conflict

So what happens when your personal brand diverges from what the company wants you to do? If you have thoughtfully crafted your personal brand statement and avoidance statements, and aren't in a role that's a complete misfit, then this shouldn't happen often. When this is likely to happen is during the management change, or an organizational restructuring, or during times when the company is experiencing a downturn. It's at these times when roles and responsibilities can get changed in radical ways, and suddenly skills and qualities are valued differently than they used to be. There can be changes that will happen in the work you're being asked to do that may diverge from the personal brand you've been cultivating. This could be a cause for conflict, and you have to carefully navigate the situation. You will likely have to make a hard choice. You can do what they are asking for the sake of getting along, in exchange for feeling like you have security in your job (which we've already covered is generally a façade) or you can look for another job.

It's a tough position, but do your best to avoid short-term conflict, trying to understand the background of the radical shifts. Based on what you are learning about these radical changes, take a step back, and determine if your personal brand statement and avoidance statements could be adjusted to still benefit you in the new environment. If they can be, this is great news, as you will experience only a minor bump in the road. At best, you can continue to build off the efforts you have already put into telling your story. If you are not able to attenuate your personal brand story to the new responsibilities, it would be an important signal that it will require significantly more effort for you to get more out of the company than they are getting out of you. Don't rush to judgment, but you will need to begin considering whether the role you are in is the right match for you and where you want to be.

Throughout this entire book, we've been giving you the tools—whether you knew it or not—to establish what your personal brand is about. If you remember from a few chapters back, we talked about staying a step ahead. If you're working on your long-term plan, likely, you're not choosing projects that suck. And if you are not executing on other people's ideas, then you're executing on yours and owning your brand, and actively building it. Even when "playing the game," you should be recognizing that you still have to do things to socialize your personal brand. We've given you the tools to make sure when you do create your personal brand, you have the building blocks to do it and the foundation to maximize it for your benefit. Without these tools, you wouldn't be effectively executing on your personal brand creation, and will likely have an identity forced on you.

Spending time developing and cultivating your personal brand and putting in the time, effort, and energy, so everyone understands it, may be one of the most important keys to getting more out of your company than they get out of you. You'll work on projects you enjoy more, which automatically results in delivering higher quality work, and it will help you get projects and experiences that match up to the skills you ultimately want to build. On top of those great things, it will build your confidence like nothing else.

TAKE HOME LESSONS:
- A personal brand is one of the single most impactful things you can do to establish control of your career and get more from your company than they get from you.
- Developing a personal brand statement and avoidance statement are critical, but worthless if you don't also make the effort to spread your message to others.
- If your personal brand deviates significantly from what the company or your manager needs, often after a reorganization or managerial change, first reevaluate if you can tweak it, and if not consider whether the role and company are still the right place for you.

ACTION ITEMS:
- Write your personal brand statement.
- Write your avoidance statement.
- Practice both, so they roll off the tongue and sound natural.
- Plan out your strategy for how, where, and when you will tell others what you are about.

CHAPTER XII
FINAL WORDS OF ADVICE...

There are two types of people in this world. One type lets the world push them around, AND the other makes the world their oyster. And if you are here, reading the final chapter of this book, it's obvious which one you are.

This book has given you the secret that organizations will never tell you, something your CEO and other leaders all know but can't say: to get the most out of your career, you have to be selfish. Whether it's getting promotions, having more freedom in your role, or being able to have the confidence that you will find a great job on your timetable because of the great value you can bring, you have to prioritize yourself over every company, every boss, every colleague.

The other truth is, all executives are calculating. In fact, most executives are already doing the things you've read about in this book or did them to get there. The closer I've worked with upper-level management, the more I've seen them putting themselves first. But by the time they get to this level of management, they've learned not to say these things. They're supposed to pretend it's all about the 'corporate mission' or 'doing the right thing for the company' and not really let on that many of the ways they achieved success had nothing to do with that. More likely, they got to their position by focusing on developing their own skills, watching closely for opportunities, and making sure that they were their own best advocate. *Then*, adopted a love for the corporate mission.

This book is all about not getting distracted or fooled by the 'propaganda' of companies that are focused on their bottom line, or for that matter, anyone else who has figured out the secret to success is to be selfish. Companies are very good at delivering their vision to you, and they want you to believe that if you align with it, it will be in your best interest— but in reality, it is designed to get the maximum out of you, without having to give you the same in return. We could even go so far as to say that the only reason companies care about talent development is because the cost of hiring and training new people is more than the cost of retaining them. Someone has to tell you the hard truth, and a CEO won't do it. A CEO isn't allowed to write this book— they're writing books to get six-figure speaking engagements. They can't say anything risky, because they have to manage their persona inside their company and their public one in the world. When was the last time you saw a book from a well-known CEO that took a radical stance or said something innovative? I'm just a lower level exec that people often ignore while I build a lifestyle that is rewarding in a number of ways. Nobody cares if I say something that gets people thinking. And if they do, I guarantee it's because it's too close for comfort for their liking.

So, before I release you back into the corporate world, let's recap some of the most important lessons I hope you've gleaned from the book.

The first thing you learned was how being a good corporate citizen may hurt you, because you will be picking up the slack of others, which takes away from you focusing on activities that truly benefit you. We discussed how to avoid becoming a Corporate Drone and instead learning to play the game by telling important people what they want to hear. We reviewed the dangers of sharing your true feelings or being fooled into thinking your manager is anything but a company mouthpiece, no matter how much they appear to care about you, your development, or your career. We talked about how focusing on promotions rather than strategically building skills can cause you to become pigeonholed or trapped at your company because you've lost touch with broad skills that are valuable at a lot of other employers. And we gave the reasons why focusing on developing your external network is more important than your internal one, and makes job hunting or advancing your career much easier.

During the middle of the book, we transitioned to more advanced techniques such as never bringing another person's idea to reality and outwitting your peers and leaders by allocating time to building a long-term plan that puts you in the driver's seat and others in reactive mode. We gave an overview of the techniques that conflict with many people's natural inclinations. You should change groups every 3 to 4 years to learn new things and to not get caught fixing previous mistakes during times when you were learning new skills. The toughest situation is knowing when to leave a sinking ship, even though everyone around you is trying to convince you to stay and help them through the misery. It's only slightly harder than diagnosing, managing, and then leaving a bad boss as they play mind games to convince you that you are the problem and not them. But remember…you aren't the problem. The only problem to solve is how quickly you can leave.

Lastly, we found out why building a new personal brand and identity is critical to your professional success and will propel you into unexpected opportunities if you truly change your identity and habits.

What wasn't in this book? This book doesn't contain one piece of advice that trades your success at the expense of others. A lot of people get to the top this way. But it comes with a variety of downsides. People doing that are taking shortcuts that will lead to a lot of problems down the road, some that may be unrecoverable—and some that they will have to face on their deathbed. That behavior isn't 'Selfish,' it's just narcissistic.

Being selfish in your career counter-intuitively makes you *more* valuable to your company. That's the biggest secret of all. The more skills you have, the more you can add. But it also gives you choices in case the situation is bad or doesn't align with your personal brand or your unique skills. Life is too short to not love your job. And having a Selfish Career makes sure you love all parts of your life equally.

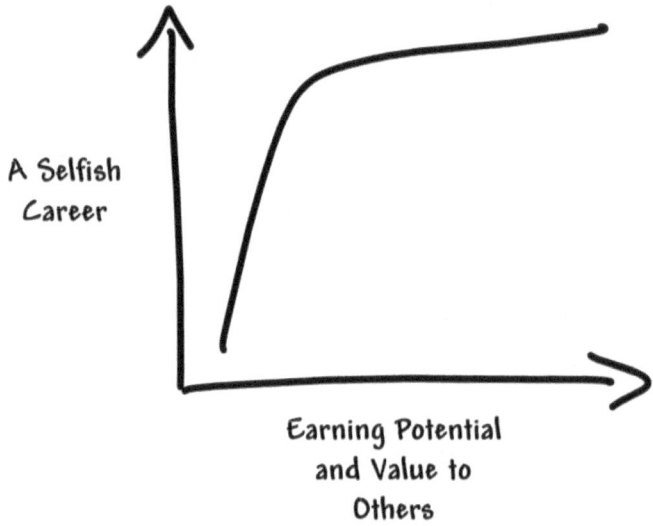

So, you now have the tools and the roadmap, but there is one thing that will stand in your way. Be mindful that you are your own best advocate and champion. You must be thoughtful in all you do. And for some people, that's too hard. But for those who want success and can think like an executive, not an underling, it provides a great framework.

Your run-of-the-mill leaders and executives will tell you to read the same old books like *Strength Finders, Lean In,* or *The 7 Habits of Highly Effective People*. I've read every one of those books, and there are spectacular nuggets of wisdom in each of them. But this is a very different point of view, and it may change how you think about your career and put you in a position where you finally have more professional options.

Not only am I drawing from my own experiences, I've taught these techniques to most of my staff, and watched them execute against their long-term plans with amazing success. One was an intern I hired that was making high five figures a year out of grad school. I worked with him consistently on building his greater skill set and not just grabbing every project he could get his hands on. He employed these techniques and moved into a job making nearly double within three months. After a while he realized he wasn't getting enough opportunities and wasn't learning anything new or advancing. He used his skills to consult on the side and after about a year, he went to work for a new company, and he's making a lot more—at least another $1/3^{rd}$ more than his previous salary. Because he was 'selfish,' and didn't become a Corporate Drone, in a year and a half, he more than doubled his income.

After many years in the corporate trenches, I have come to realize that the only advocate I can trust is myself, and the only thing holding you back is you. It's all about carving out a new identity for yourself. We've called that Selfish, but that's what it is. These are tactics for navigating your job while you're developing that new identity. The goal isn't to stick it out for twenty years at one place, the goal is maximizing your opportunities at large to benefit you and your family. Not everyone is going to do this, and that's a good thing. It wouldn't be good if everyone was selfish. But for the people who need this information, it's great. This is for the person who believes in themselves more than their company seems to believe in them. And the person that recognizes that the days of companies watching out for their employees are long over. It's the perfect set of tools for maximizing opportunities for income and building skills that makes them more valuable over the long run.

In conclusion, you now have all the rule benders so you can make sure you're getting more out of your career than the company is getting out of you. The concepts in this book and the rules that have been laid out are not that difficult to understand, but they can be very difficult to execute. And that's because it is human nature to fall into a pattern of comfort and to have a desire for predictability, safety, and reliability. Unfortunately, the current job market doesn't provide you predictability, safety, or reliability. People are expendable, and corporations have designed advanced methods to get the most out of human resources, and often to their detriment. Hard work isn't enough; I've found that to be true. You must be selfish.

I hope with this new knowledge you go into your job with a new perspective focused on getting the most out of every opportunity, so you can have the greatest number of options. I want you to maximize every moment of time at your company, building skills that will help you advance through the organization, and give you a chance at a much higher level of control over your day-to-day life. Skill development and racking up experiences will lay the groundwork. Maybe that's working for a big company or going out on your own. But the greatest value you could achieve executing the strategies in this book would be a life where professional anxiety is lowered, allow you to set more boundaries, control of your day, or spend more time living the type of life we should all want. And that's a life with our families, friends, and the pursuits of our passions.

www.ingramcontent.com/pod-product-compliance
Lightning Source LLC
Chambersburg PA
CBHW032009170526
45157CB00002B/618